FORT WORTH PUBLIC LIBRARY

Y0-CDN-327

Tracks to Murder

364.1523 GOODMAN 2005
Goodman, Jonathan
Tracks to murder

Central

JUL 1 8 2006

CENTRAL LIBRARY

TRUE CRIME SERIES
Albert Borowitz, Editor

Tracks to Murder

Jonathan Goodman

The Kent State University Press

KENT AND LONDON

© 2005 The Kent State University Press, Kent, Ohio 44242
ALL RIGHTS RESERVED
Library of Congress Catalog Card Number 2004026038
ISBN 0-87338-825-9
Manufactured in the United States of America

Unless otherwise noted, all illustrations are from the author's collection.

Designed by Christine Brooks and set in 9.7/14 Stone Serif. Printed by Sheridan Books, Inc.

09 08 07 06 05   5 4 3 2 1

LIBRARY OF CONGRESS CATALOGING-IN-PUBLICATION DATA
Goodman, Jonathan.
    Tracks to murder / Jonathan Goodman.
        p.   cm.— (True crime series (Kent, Ohio))
    Includes index.
    ISBN 0-87338-825-9 (pbk. : alk. paper) ∞
    1. Murder—United States—Case studies. I. Title. II. Series.
    HV6529.G66 2005
    364. 152'3'0973—dc22   2004026038

British Library Cataloging-in-Publication data are available.

For William Hildebrand and Dean Keller,
who put me on the right lines

Contents

The Reasons Why

A s is so, I believe, with most Big Moments in most people's lives, the one that sparked a large part of my destiny, of being a crime historian, did not seem big when it happened. The thought that it might not have happened—that, considering the circumstances, it shouldn't have—still sometimes gives me the unsettling feeling that perhaps the notion of ordained fate is not to be scoffed at.

The Moment was of the late 1950s. That I cannot be more exact goes to show how uninfluential it seemed at the time and for a long while afterward. I was the stage director, occasionally, precociously, *the* director, at the Liverpool Playhouse, home of that seaside city's repertory company, the oldest in the world (since the eleventh day of the eleventh month of 1911—even I, with my now ramshackle memory, have no trouble remembering that). It was usual after the evening show— though not on Thursdays or Saturdays, when there was a matinee as well as a morning rehearsal, leaving us all dog-tired (a fact that at least reduces the days of the week for the Big Moment by a third)—for some of us to gather in the green room or in the band room under the stage, either just to chat over a bottle of wine or to play poker or pontoon for penny stakes. But at ten or so on *that* night, a guest actor, Geoffrey Edwards, sauntered into my room and said words to this effect:

"If you're in no hurry to get back to your digs, why don't we take a look at 29 Wolverton Street?"

I said something like "What's so special about Wolverton Street—extra-special about Number 29?"—and he, as if auditioning for the role of Mystery Man, said something like "I'll explain when we get there."

How we got there I cannot remember—any more than why I so pliantly agreed to go. It must have been by bus. To the drab suburb called Anfield. Through side streets of small, grubby terraced houses to another that seemed no different. Wolverton Street. And now I was being told (with respect to Geoffrey Edwards, a touch overdramatically) what made Number 29 worth coming specially to see—what set it apart from all other houses anywhere. It—its front room (which my memory assures me, probably imaginatively, was masked from us by red velvet curtains)—was the scene of the killing of Mrs. Julia Wallace on the night of Tuesday, January 20, 1931: the starting-off point, Geoffrey Edwards told me (and he was not exaggerating), of the most fascinating of all criminous riddles—a whodunit, still officially unsolved, that, though fashioned into fiction by several novelists, was beyond the wit of any of them, or any others, to improve. I feel safe in saying that, tucked somewhere into his monologue, there was the quote about truth being stranger than fiction.

Years went by. For the first half dozen of them, I continued working in the theater: after Liverpool as *the* director with other repertory companies, with touring shows, with West End productions that didn't run. Then into television, where, though I had hardly even watched any of it, let alone learned anything about its technicalities, I was straightway appointed sole producer of a weekly fictional-crime series that, probably not because it was eminently worth watching but because fewer of the millions of TV addicts wanted to watch the programs that were on at the same time, was always high in the national ratings; meanwhile, mainly because my script editor, formerly a police detective, was even less suited to his new job than I was to mine but couldn't be fired, owing to the fact that he had been given the job as a thank you from a top executive whom he had helped out of a criminal scrape, I sometimes needed to scribble a script because none was ready for the next episode, which meant that, for the first time, I wrote pseudonymously (I had by then had books published and stage plays produced under my own name), usually as William Walter, my middle names, but occasionally as a bizarre anagram, Damon Jon Gothana, that didn't fool anyone.

During that time, I had married (I am now divorced, a state that is mostly the fault of the selfishness that I prefer to call single-mindedness), and throughout that time, since the nocturnal sightseeing in Wolverton Street, the Wallace case had been stuck like a burr to the back of my mind, sometimes being detached to the front of it by references to the case in books on true crime that, after the sightseeing, I had taken to reading lots of.

Believing—wrongly, as it turned out—that with the money saved from my television earnings as a producer and as a forced laborer on scripts, I could afford to take time off, sufficient to research and write a book on the Wallace case; I became self-employed. Three years later the script of *The Killing of Julia Wallace* was accepted by a London publisher, and eighteen months afterward (so long a time because of a legal problem that at one nerve-racking point threatened to scupper publication) the book appeared. Excepting a couple of years, it has been in print, latterly with revisions, ever since.

And also ever since, I have written one book overlappingly after another—at first, until early in the 1980s, during hours left over from being managing editor of a publishing firm that specialized in subjects I knew nothing about (as I had found as a TV producer, ignorance can be an advantage, letting one see elementary nonsenses that experts either haven't noticed, often through being blinded by jargon, or wouldn't dare question in case they could be blamed for them), and then, following a final bust-up with my so-called partner, a congenitally potty expatriate Austrian who had become completely crazy after a frontal lobotomy, as a full-time author. I am certainly not proud of the sheer number of books, most on true crimes, that I have published in the latter, continuing period, but I am grateful that I have been able to publish that many, for the pot-boiling three quarters of them (each, I plead, containing *something* of value) have subsidized the research and writing of the relative few that I felt were *needed,* that I would be sorry not to have written (which is not to say that I am quite satisfied with any of those; the best one can do can always be bettered later—always when it is too late).

Guessing your question: Why have I told you all that—all that about myself? Well, for the simple reason that two friends, William Hildebrand and Dean Keller (you will meet them, far too briefly, in this book), have told me that I must, have told me that some before-the-facts explanations are required—reasons why I, an Englishman, am taking a trip by rail (why rail?) of some six thousand miles, west from New York to the Pacific, then looping back along more southerly lines, with stopovers in eight cities and at a place that none of the Americans to whom I have mentioned it (and they are all good at geography) has ever heard of.

It was not until I was told that explanations were needed that, causing a despairing shake of the head at myself, I realized that I had not given half enough thought to what all of them were. What instantly occurred to me was that I had never been farther west in America than a few miles beyond Cleveland, Ohio—but just as instantly I saw that that explanation shouldn't be one, for the notion that it is sensible to go somewhere simply because you have never been there makes no sense whatever, except to the travel agent who tries to persuade you that it does. When one thinks of most of the places one hasn't been to, it becomes clear that one hasn't been to them because they aren't worth going to—and the saying about travel, that it broadens the mind, doesn't bear scrutiny, is knocked on the head by the fact that retired long-distance lorry drivers are unlikely to have minds broader than those of little old car-less ladies living in bus-less villages where they were born, their main association with the outside world being travelogues on television.

But I do have what seem to me good reasons for going to particular places west and roughly south of Cleveland. In each of those places a murder happened, all a long while ago—not just any old murder, no thud-and-blunder affair, but one that is worth remembering, rarely because of the crime itself but because of strangenesses arising from, or brought to light by, that crime. A good many of those strangenesses were not at all strange when the cases made front-page news but have become so because of what is known as progress—and they, it seems to me, are more helpful toward gathering how it *felt* to be living in certain places in certain years than all the footnotes in all the social-history tomes put together. Amending the start of L. P. Hartley's *The Go-Between* slightly, "The past is a foreign country; they did things differently there."

It helps—me, at any rate—to *see* those places. And that, after all, is no different from visiting Gettysburg to see and feel where Lincoln made that speech of his, to wander around Thomas Hardy's home, to stand where Rembrandt stood and conjured art.

Perhaps you are now beginning to understand why I spoke earlier, several times, of the Wallace case. I am positive that if I had not been persuaded that night so long ago to take the trip specially to see 29 Wolverton Street, I would not, years later, have been determined to do everything possible toward knowing why Julia Wallace was killed, whether her husband (found guilty by a jury but released by the Court of Criminal Appeal) was the culprit, and if it were shown that he was innocent—a second victim of the crime—whether there was evidence indicating the identity of the killer. If I had not written that book, I would not have become, as it were, typecast as a crime historian. My life would have taken a quite different turning or would not have turned at all—and the thought of what might not have been gives me the shivers, for, never minding the problems and disappointments of what I do, I would not want to do anything else. I am astonished that I have been and still am so fortunate.

Corollary to what I said just now, it is not possible to write surely about a crime that happened, no matter how long ago, in a place one has never visited. How can anyone convey the essence of the Crippen case (as much a love story as a tale of murder) if he has not ridden on the top deck of a London bus from Oxford Circus to Holloway, or conjure up the atmosphere among the English colony near Nairobi at the time of the murder of Lord Erroll if his awareness of the place is inflated from picture postcards of Happy Valley, or evoke the local chatterings regarding Miss Lizzie Borden if he knows Fall River no more intimately than as a dot on a map of Massachusetts? Although such rhetorical questions are not expectant of answers, I must state that the single answer to those and similar ones is that *no one possibly can*—and, further to that answer, that anyone who tries to is, by definition, a lazy researcher, not really a researcher at all, and therefore not to be bothered with, let alone given the benefit of doubts about the truths of his account.

On this trip of mine it won't matter if, at some of the places I visit, the scene of the crime, the scenery of it, has changed. Perhaps all the better, for as long as one's imagination knows boundaries, with warnings of how far and where not to go, it often snaps clearer pictures than does the contraption called a Sure Shot I shall have with me—please God (maybe I should have mentioned that I am a lazy Quaker, also that I am rather absentminded), till the end.

Other reasons for the trip? Well, yes, several—among them, the way I am taking it: by train. No romantic steam any longer . . . but never mind: I can pretend the sight—and just as easily, the smell, the sound—of it. There will be occasions, I'm sure, when those cloudy pretenses will come in handy, given that no more than a few of the murder cases that I shall, so to say, be visiting are of this post-steam era. The elderly itinerary reflects my general preference for cases that have stood the test of time—and that are old enough, being beyond the reach of most people's recollections, to be thought of as a kind of fiction. As I have said elsewhere, the crime historian is, basically, a novelist telling a truth. Or ought to be.

Now surely, I need delay you—myself—no longer.

Going West

Friday the Thirteenth—as it happens. The fact that it *has* happened, against my superstitious will, creates an unease on top of the perfectly natural ones at the start of a lengthy, quite complicated roundtrip that will surely provide opportunities for proving what in England, perhaps here too, is called Sod's Law: *Anything that can go wrong will go wrong.*

I am not at all embarrassed by my superstitions—half a dozen, I guess—at least one of them, which forbids conversational naming of Shakespeare's Scottish play, left over from when I worked in the theater. Most people have some, and what seems to me like most of the others are so determined to prove their unsuperstitiousness (by, for obvious example, making detours so as to walk under ladders) that they might just as well turn to voodoo or psychiatry.

The unluckiness of the number thirteen is almost official in Manhattan: thirteen is often skipped in the numbering of streets and apartment

As slang for dying, "going west" was coined in London late in the sixteenth century, referring to the westward route of the tumbrils carting condemned prisoners from Newgate Prison to the Tyburn place of execution (now Marble Arch).

blocks (on the one-sided St Luke's Place in Greenwich Village, Number 12, the home of poor Starr Faithfull until just before her mysterious death in the summer of 1931, is followed by Number 12½), and I don't know of a single skyscraper with an admitted thirteenth floor. Now that I think of it, I have never needed to visit any of the still blessedly few noticeably tall buildings in central London, and so I have no idea whether they too pretend to be thirteenth floorless. It is hard to believe that the National Westminster Bank, guilty of the tallest of them, would have permitted an inaccuracy in a numerical progression.

Constraints hemmed me in to this starting date. I thought: Set off in September by when, surely, the heat of the American summer will have abated, but not too late in the month, else by the end of the trip the days will be darkening around teatime. Once the fortnight-or-so period in which to start was decided, arrangements I had made, and arrangements made for me in and near Cleveland, my first port of call, left me with no option but to set off today.

By trying to avoid the heat, I have come here during a record-breaking heat wave. Every day since I arrived at Kennedy Airport last Sunday (meanwhile, I have stayed at Flushing with friends, Jean and Jeffrey Bloomfield—both religiously busy because, without my prior knowledge, now is the time of Rosh Hashanah, the Jewish new year), the temperature has soared, soggy with humidity, to the mid-nineties.

Even now, shortly before seven in the evening, and though this custard-colored waiting area in Pennsylvania Station is windowless and a long ramp away from the street, the air is like the stuff that comes out of those press-button machines in public lavatories that, if you have a quarter of an hour to spare, dry your hands almost as efficiently as would a paper towel.

I wish I had seen—experienced—the *real* Penn Station: a place of beauty as well as splendor—an undangerously exciting place too. But by the time I first came to New York (a look through expired passports and the present one—all confirming that I'm British; the next will class me as a mere European, lumped in with such nice people as Lithuanians and erstwhile East Germans—has reminded me that my first visit was in 1976 and that, though instantly entranced by Manhattan, I have only been able to come here twenty-four times since) the real Penn Station had been destroyed, and this ticky-tacky replacement, stuck beneath the vandals' office block and the concrete toad-stool they had had the cheek to call Madison Square Garden, was already a slum.

This place has associations—broken associations—with the great architect Stanford White. It was his firm that designed the real Penn Station. And it was he who designed the original Madison Square Garden, "the most magnificent amusement palace in the world," which embellished the corner of Madison Avenue and 26th Street, some distance from the namesake thing upstairs. That building had a rooftop theater, and it was there in the summer of 1906, during the first night of a musical called *Mamzelle Champagne*—a comedian was singing "I Could Love a Million Girls"—that the rich maniac Harry K. Thaw, made even crazier by the suspicion that his dolly-bird wife, Evelyn, had been seduced by Stanford White, sidled through the audience to where the architect was sitting and shot him to death. Perhaps the heat of the day has addled my mind, but I think there is a similarity between the killing of an artist by a mad millionaire and the destruction of a living work of art by a gang of money-mad financiers.

Rooftop theaters were all the rage in Manhattan at one time: a symptom of the fact that, as the borough is an island, its acreage finite, there was a need, so far as many financiers were concerned, to "think tall" and to ensure that every cubic inch of architectural space was profitably employed. None of the rooftop theaters remains (I suppose because of lately more-stringent fire regulations), and I know of only one surviving building capped by rooftop-theater space, that being the New Amsterdam Theater on 42nd Street, a miracle of Art Nouveau: Florenz Ziegfeld's "palace of entertainment" from before the Great War till the end of the 1920s. Like most of the rest of the stretch of 42nd Street to the west of Times Square, the main off-the-sidewalk New Amsterdam Theater was for years used sleazily—as a porn-movie cinema frequented by sad and unimaginative people incapable of masturbating without visual aid—but the building lay derelict for a long while.

The New Amsterdam's rooftop theater was the setting for salient incidents in the Elwell murder case of 1920, and while I was doing the research for a book called *The Slaying of Joseph Bowne Elwell* the kindly owners of the New Amsterdam agreed to let me look around the rooftop theater—easier said than done on the morning when I arrived, for the caretaker, a revival of Groucho Marx, even down to the accessory of a cigar as large as his moustache, either hadn't been told to expect me or was extravagantly suspicious by nature. My efforts toward convincing him of my inoffensiveness seemed only to make his rejections of them more surreal—still more so when, trying to annul his comment that for all he knew I was carrying a bomb, I suggested that he should search me, and he backed away, squealing, "Oh yeah?—and get blown to bits?—me as macaroni?" Since I drew the line at undressing in an open doorway on that part of 42nd Street, his remark perfectly illustrated the difficulty of proving a negative. But perhaps my continual but carefully casual dropping of the names, the first names, of his bosses did the trick: he suddenly relented and, though still jittery, zoomed me up to the roof in one of the ornate elevators, then shadowed me, the smoke from his cigar fogging my view, as I pottered around the galleried, sky-lit place where Ziegfeld presented a score of editions of his *Midnight Frolics:* where packed audiences, all in full fig, laughed at the carefully rehearsed adlibbing of Will Rogers and the eye-rolling of Eddie Cantor, joined in the chorus of "Secondhand Rose" with "Funny Girl" Fanny (subsequently—more elegantly—Fannie) Brice, and gaped at the glamour and the glamorous costumes of the showgirls. Despite the fog and the unkempt emptiness, it was easy to imagine the place as it wonderfully used to be.

Thank the Lord—that crackle from the loudspeaker, the stampede toward the guarded gate, must mean that the train is ready for boarding.

I have a brand new suitcase, bought because it is light and has casters, and a satchel. I am wearing moleskin trousers—not because they really are of moleskin, so an obtrusive label says, but because they have six deep pockets, four at the front, two of them with flaps, and two flapped ones at the back. I need all six to carry and keep apart (1) loose change, (2) hankie, (3) train tickets, which are just like the airline sort, and sleeper reservation cards, (4) travelers' checks, (5) the form listing the numbers of the checks, and (6) a little, black leatherette notebook—"With Compliments of Taj Mahal Tandoori, Ealing Common, London W5," which is my local take-out restaurant. And I still need the inside pockets of my brown tweed jacket, one for my passport (banks won't cash travelers' checks without it) and the other for my wallet, plump with all sorts of things, including paper money and credit cards. I don't expect to remember which of the eight pockets contains what, and I know that every so often I shall stick something with something else and then, a little while later, pat the empty pocket and get a fright.

Yesterday morning, on the subway train from Flushing Main Street to Grand Central (its concourse more splendid than many cathedral naves; the vandals, several times repelled, are no doubt biding their time), I was sitting on the right-hand side of a space-for-two seat facing the aisle. A little Hispanic chap, wearing a neat gray suit and proper shoes, got on at the Shea Stadium stop. He was, I observed, one-armed; his left sleeve was limp, the cuff tucked into the pocket. He sat beside me. After a few more stops, I felt a rummaging in the region of my left-hand back pocket. I was perplexed—and, after a moment more of the rummaging, queasy, for as my neighbor's one arm was visible across his lap, I could only imagine that some small furry creature had nibbled its way through the back of the seat and would soon be nibbling *me*. Reacting without further thought, I banged my left elbow down into the gap, which caused the little man to let out a squeal—more from pain than surprise, because (I didn't realize this yet) I had probably fractured the wrist on the arm he hadn't appeared to have. He jumped up and scampered, whimpering the while, to the end of the coach and through the door to the next one—and, I suppose, through others— till at the next stop he got off. Even while I could still have seen him, I had noticed that my Taj Mahal Tandoori notebook, wallet-like to the touch, was lying on the seat beside me, and I was understanding that he had contorted his hidden arm behind his back so as to pick my pocket. I felt several emotions; perhaps oddly, the strongest was relief that the rummaging had not been by a rodent.

Afterward, while considering the incident (the first time, so far as I know, that anyone in America has tried to rob me), I decided that the little man, with his presumably novel idea of one-armed banditry, proved my maxim that the best ideas occur to people who don't know how to use them, and I remembered a television commercial, I never noticed what it advertised, in which an old lady, visiting Manhattan, asked a workman in a hard hat how she could get to Carnegie Hall, and he advised her, "Practice, ma'am, practice."

I have never understood why, whereas British railway stations have platforms, most American ones have sidewalks, therefore requiring stepstools for getting on and off the trains. This means that, saving staff the bother of putting down dozens of stools, no more than a few doors are used; also that, probably in accordance with some safety regulation, each used door has an attendant to flutter a reassuring hand near passengers' elbows and to help with their lighter items of luggage. Usually it also means that the nearest usable door is some miles from one's seat.

Not for me tonight, though: this train has only one carriage of seat-cum-sleeper compartments ("roomettes," they are called), and there is a particular door to it. The sleeper attendant, who is black (I notice later that none of the passengers he attends to is), is more conspicuously vast; he has to walk sideways along the corridor but still grazes the compartments on both sides. Having located my compartment, he stows my case on the high shelf, places my satchel on one of the two facing bench seats, and is already reciting a little speech, explaining where things are and how things work, and ending, "My name is Sidney, sir, and it will be my sincere pleasure to accommodate your every wish." He loiters at the doorway, and I don't know if he is waiting, like a genie, for my first wish or is expecting a tip.

Tipping: one of the small worries, separated into smaller ones, when traveling abroad—whom to tip (more than once I have offended by offering a tip to someone who did not consider himself a servant); how much to give when there is no bill to work out a percentage of; having the right coin or note, for it is embarrassing to ask for change (I used to have a maiden aunt who never went anywhere, not even to tea at the local Fuller's, without a second handbag containing, I suppose among other things, a copy of her will, a bottle of smelling salts, a tiny tin of lavender-scented cachous [not for her own use but to offer to adjacent acquaintances suffering from even the merest hint of halitosis], a roll of tissue-paper haloes for putting on lavatory seats—and a purse of tipping coins: two of each, ranging from threepenny bit to half-crown). As for Sidney—and other sleeper attendants on subsequent trains—I don't know whether one is expected to tip for each helpfulness or lavish a lump sum at the end. While I am wondering about that, Sidney, looking sincerely undisappointed, closes the sliding-glass door between us.

Before sitting down, I light a cigarette—my first for nearly an hour, because smoking was forbidden in the waiting area (though some of the people there did smoke; I gathered from whiffs that not all of the cigarettes were of tobacco). Antismoking campaigners have had more success in America than in England. Allowing that the cause is good, I must say that its spokesmen—those I have seen on television at home, none wearing a tie and all as aggressive as ardent pacifists—seem to prove a law I have made up: *good causes attract bad advocates.* I equate them with religious fundamentalists. And with vegans.

I want to believe what I read recently, that vegans, who are generally scared stiff about damage to the ozone layer, may be widening holes in it by their excessive farting, far more destructive than emissions from those aerosol air fresheners they have helped to get banned. If there is not already a society of vegans in England, where pressure groups make up the largest growth industry, I am sure there soon will be one, probably with a royal warrant. It could, in that case, be called the Royal Society of Vegan People, RSVP for short. And, just as there is now a retaliatory anti-anti-smokers society, there could be a Society for the Protectors of Eaters of Red Meat (SPERM, of course), with a motto borrowed from Pythagoras: *Abstineto a fabis,* which translates as the environmentally friendly warning, "Abstain from beans."

The walls of this roomette are patched with little signs, cautionary, descriptive, explanatory; even the ashtrays have instructions. "Used Blades" explains what a tiny slit near the folded-up washbasin, itself with instructions, was intended for. The slit goes to show that this carriage was made at least thirty years ago, before plastic-cartridge blades began to replace the simple, double-bladed ones that gave more shaves. Ergo, the carriage must be pre-Amtrak—"Amtrak" being the abbreviated name of the body that runs what it is careful not to call the *nationalized* intercity passenger railroad. I read from a "source book," one of the things I have received from people in Amtrak's public affairs department (very helpful people, though still not as helpful as those employed by Amtrak's agent in London, a firm called Destination Marketing):

Rail passenger transportation, which was the principal mode of transportation in this nation before World War II, had fallen to just four percent of inter-city travel by 1958. Faced with tough competition from air travel and private automobile use, most private rail carriers chose not to invest new capital in passenger cars and facilities, causing service to deteriorate during the 1960s. In 1970, Congress decided to preserve and revive a national rail passenger system with the passage of the Rail Passenger Corporation, better known as Amtrak, a private company incorporated under the laws of the District of Columbia.

I glance at the window and am somewhat surprised, even slightly confused, to find that this train is moving—and must have been moving for some minutes, for it has already emerged from the Penn Station tunnel and is traveling past places I recognize as being in the direction of Harlem. I didn't hear any warning whistles or shouts, wasn't aware of a starting lurch—and even now, though we're going at a fair speed, I can only feel movement when I concentrate on feeling it.

All of a sudden, I am happy. Part of the happiness is from having escaped from Penn; part is sybaritic, of the this-is-the-life sort; part, the largest part, is from knowing that I am on my way not just to a city, Cleveland, but to friends whom I haven't seen for almost a year.

All of the long-distance routes have names. This one, which goes on (as I shall) from Cleveland to Chicago, used to have the most famous of American train names, the Twentieth Century Limited (Ben Hecht and Charles MacArthur wrote a play set along its lines, and a musical based on the play was a Broadway success in the late 1970s), but the name has been changed to Lake Shore Limited. Trying to imagine why, I wonder if the pre-Amtrak company claimed possession of the Twentieth Century as a trade name, rather as the Warner Brothers claimed, though unsuccessfully, that as they had made a movie called *Casablanca,* the Marx Brothers could not spend *A Night* in there.

By now we have passed through the wasteland of Harlem and of the Bronx (the home in the 1930s of the enigmatic Dr. J. F. Condon— "Jafsie"—of the Lindbergh kidnapping case, who described the Bronx he knew as "the most beautiful borough in the world"); Yonkers also is behind us, and the window shows scenery. It is getting dark as we come alongside the Hudson River, which will be there on the left for more than a hundred miles; the ribbon reflection of the sunset is brighter than the sunset itself. I experience déjà vu and, for once, know the cause: the window is the repeated window shot of sunset over the Hudson in those early scenes of *North by Northwest,* which is my favorite among the several Hitchcock movies that use trains (which, come to think of it, are my favorite Hitchcock movies). Excepting the Wild West train-robbery sort, I cannot think of a single movie that has a murder on an *American* train.

And, with the same exception, none of the American crime historians I have asked knows of any such real-life crime. There have been plenty in England—sufficient for me, some years ago, to compile a sizeable anthology of accounts of not all of them. The main reason for the geographical imbalance is that, while American carriages, apart from this sleeper sort, have always been undivided, until quite recently most English ones were of compartments, which sometimes offered an opportunity for murder to be done discreetly.

Changing the subject in my mind, I think of another train scene in *North by Northwest*—of Roger O. Thornhill's comment, not referring mainly to rail travel: "Beats flying, doesn't it?" Accepting that, at my age, any remote chance of using the comment double meaningly is past, I make sure that neither Sidney nor anyone less apparent is passing the door and say it aloud.

Although I am not really hungry, I decide to have a bit of dinner. The restaurant car is almost empty; the mess-jacketed waiters, all of them black, outnumber the customers. Thinking that I should like to be by a window on the other side from my roomette, I start to sit at an empty table in a line of also empty ones, but the head man orders me to sit at a specific one of the empty tables across the aisle. I obey, and before long a waiter approaches, asks me how I'm doing, and drops a printed form on the table.

His Christian name, I see from his lapel badge, is Gay (which, for most men, would be troublesome—it is a shame that homosexuals, with so many equivocal words to choose from, commandeered a word that was perfectly precise, without alternative; strangely, the meaning of the noun *gaiety* remains, in England at any rate, intact). Gay advises me to go for "the special" and, when I ask what "the special" is, says that if I really want to know, he will enquire of the chef. I tell him not to bother and (by ticking boxes on the form) order Caesar salad, cuttle-fish with trimmings, banana cake, regular coffee, and, asking Gay to bring it with the salad, white wine.

A young man, blond, wearing a smart gray suit, appears from the direction of the roomettes, starts to sit at an empty table, and is sent to join me. Gay, who hasn't left, gives him a form to tick, again unsuc-cessfully promotes the special, and eventually leaves, singing, not hum-ming, "I Could Have Danced All Night."

"Cabaret too," my enforced companion murmurs, and that gets us talking. He tells me that he has spent a few days in New York after attending a conference in Washington, D.C., and is on his way to an-other conference in Dallas. I guess that he is a salesman only because all of the salesmen I know seem to spend more time conferring than selling. But I am wrong, quite surprisingly wrong. He is a nurse. Not-ing my attempt to appear unsurprised, he says that, "according to a recent data gather, as many as 4 percent of nurses are male." While I am trying to make sense of that, for I find percentages almost as mean-ingless as averages (a man who for some reason had his feet in an oven and his head in a refrigerator, when asked how he felt, replied that, on average, he was quite comfortable), he adds, not just to my surprise but to my astonishment, that he is "a neonatal nurse practitioner." I say, "You mean that you . . . er . . ." and he says, "Sure," which is not a satisfactory answer to the question I didn't know how to finish.

Without explaining why I tell him about the only time I was in hospital, for a hernia operation. My fear before the operation was as nothing compared with the terror on mornings after, when the hernia-specializing surgeon, whose name (I swear it) was Mr. Slack, came to my bedside with a party of interns that included, always at the front, two seemingly teenaged girls and, employing what I am sure was a dipstick, tapped vicinities of my usually private parts, all the time say-ing things in medical language that made one of the girls beam with delight and the other peer with fascination—and I, trying to look non-chalant, even debonair, *knew* that the next tap, slightly off target, would cause the genital equivalent of a knee-jerk reaction, misinterpreted by all the sightseers. I get as far as telling the neonatal nurse practitioner that what I knew would happen never did, when he interrupts, saying that he takes my point but that, in his professional experience of maternity, he has never, not once, encountered "patient resistance" on account of his maleness.

We talk of other, for me less controversial, things. He—having, as is the usual American way, had his coffee served at the start of the meal—is finished first and leaves. I drink some coffee and the last of the wine—which, though labeled White Zinfandel, is rosé colored—and stroll back to the roomette.

I may as well get to bed—and only now do I consider the umpteen preparations toward doing that and the order of making them. First of all, close the curtain across the glass door, and then, in no imperative order, use the wash basin and loo—which, worryingly, once the bed has been folded down, can't be used—get undressed and into pajamas, hang clothes in the hanger-wide wardrobe, and collect together what I shall or may need once I'm in bed. And then, holding those things in one hand, open the curtain and the door and, leaning in from the corridor, fold down the bed, which fits wall to wall, clamber up and onto it (easier said than done for short people, who must need a leg-up, from the sleeping partner if the roomette is being shared or from the attendant), and close the door and curtain.

I have done all that—and now realize that there is something that I should have done: worked out which switch is which in a recess so tucked away in a jamb of the door that, from bed level, it is out of sight. Fumbling, I turn a switch that makes the air-conditioning yodel, another, which accelerates the fan in the ceiling to such an extent that the blades become the merest blur; I can see the securing screws shivering in their sockets, and I think again now particularly of Hitchcock's *Strangers on a Train,* alarmedly of the fairground scene in which the merry-go-round goes round far too fast and careens away from its moorings—and three more switches, none of which does anything apparent (though I worry for a minute, after turning the third, that I haven't noticed what in England are called communication cords, and perhaps I have started an alarm bell ringing in the driver's cabin or wherever Sidney sits)—and at long last find the switches I need, one turning the main lights off, the other turning the reading lamp on.

For trips of this lengthy sort the books for pleasure that I pack are paperbacks, for their comparative lightness, of books that I know—and know are worth their weight. This time I chose *Bleak House, The*

Great Gatsby (which I return to at least once a year, always finding fresh delights), Patrick Hamilton's *Gorse Trilogy,* and *Berlioz and His Century* by Jacques Barzun—with whom I lunched a few days ago, not at the Century Club (a Stanford White building), where we have often met, but with his wife, Marguerite, a charmer, at their apartment on Fifth Avenue, looking across Central Park toward Columbia University, which he graced for so long. Goodness me, how I treasure my friendship with him—for slightly fewer years, with them both.

I have left the four books in my bag. Intentionally. I am tired, and it would be silly to risk a skipping by the eyes or mind of any of their treats. I took from my bag a book that was given to me during the week by its publisher, Hugh Abramson, whose firm is called International Polygonics—called that, he explained, because the first book he published, not thinking of it as the first but as the one and only, had to do with geometry, and so, when he needed to think up a company name in a hurry, he invented a word that sounded geometrical and added an adjective that might make the invention seem prevalent. He has published hundreds more books, none on geometry; most are new editions of books that were long out of print, and many of those are in the fictional-crime genre.

He is a large man, both up (he is as tall as I am) and around, with hair, grown long at the back and sides of a bald pate, of that soft sort that the merest of breezes, even from the passing by of an unhurried waiter, makes ripples in. I believe that, simply because I suffer from shynesses myself, I am expert at recognizing signs of it in others. I thought I did in Hugh Abramson, and I thought at first that his fast talkativeness, never loud and sometimes, when running out of breath, a diminishing murmur, was meant to leave no space for one of those silences that embarrass new acquaintances. But—I still think he is shy—it turned out that he is naturally a fast talker and that he talks faster when talking, as he was at the start, of books that he has published, is about to, or hopes to. He seems to know every word of every one of them. I suppose most publishers love books, but I have met very few who love most of the books they publish; Hugh Abramson is the first I have met who only publishes books he loves.

The one he gave me is *Dr. Sam Johnson, Detector,* a collection of Boswell pastiches by Lillian de la Torre—whose name was already known to me because I have her true-crime books at home. I may be wrong, but I think she was the first American crime historian to write about pre-Ripper British cases. Her Johnson-qua-Holmes, Boswell-qua-Watson book, suited for bedtime reading if only by being of short stories, has become specially suited for *my* bedtime reading, for I have recently been rereading some of the real Boswell as a voluntary consequence of having talked about "the literature of crime" to sixth-formers of the King Edward VI College in the Midlands town of Stourbridge, where Johnson studied and, for a short time, taught.

After reading a few of the stories, I turned off the reading lamp and tried to sleep. Perhaps I tried too hard—perhaps there were too many diverse thoughts bumping about in my mind; anyway, I am now wide-awake. It is nearly one o'clock in the morning, and the train, which has made several stops, none for long except at Albany, where passengers from Boston boarded, is pulling into another station.

Syracuse.

It was from here on a Saturday in March 1927 that a bespectacled little man of thirty-four, as drab as his name, Judd Gray, set off for New York City, with the purpose of murder.

He was a salesman for the Bien Jolie Corset Company, and it was his work that had brought him to Syracuse. He hoped that when he returned the next day no one would have noticed his absence, and on Monday he could make the rest of his sales calls in and near Syracuse, then travel to his home in New Jersey—to his wife and daughter, both of whom he loved. Although he was going to kill for no reason other than that Mrs. Ruth Snyder wanted to be a widow, he was certainly not in love with her now, and I don't think he had ever been in love with her during the twenty months of an affair, inaugurated uncomfortably on the floor of Bien Jolie's Manhattan office after business hours, that had been carried on in hotel rooms, the costs of which Judd, leaning further from lifelong rectitude, included on his expense account. Rather, he was besotted with the *idea* that he, so drab, was attractive to an attractive blond—and when Ruth (having told him, often and always tearfully, what a monster her husband, Albert, was and that divorce was unthinkable as she had to think of her nine-year-old daughter, Lorraine, and, later on, proving to the therefore joyous Judd that she had complete trust in him, of how she had tried, not

Judd Gray, ca. 1927.

once but several times, to "get rid of the Guv'nor" as if by fatal accident) pleaded with him to commit murder on her behalf, he, terrified
of losing her, of becoming entirely drab again, pretended to be considering ways and means . . . and then made excuses for not having bought
any of the things on the shopping list she had prepared . . . and then
(she had stopped pleading, was demanding) bought all of the things:
among them, chloroform, a sash-weight, and rubber gloves . . . and
now, now that the date she had fixed had come, traveled to Grand

Ruth Snyder, ca. 1927.

Central, arriving there at 10:20 p.m., and walked through rain to Penn Station, and went on the Long Island Rail Road to Jamaica Station, and walked the mile or so to the Snyders' home, a new clapboard house in Queens Village, which Albert was buying on a mortgage that he could just about afford from his salary as the art editor of *Motor Boating* magazine.

Ruth had left the side door unlatched. She had put a cigarette packet on the kitchen table, but he couldn't remember what she had said it would mean: either that she and her husband and their daughter were still at a party or that they had returned and were upstairs. He crept up the stairs, opened doors a slit, and, finding all the rooms empty, went into the one that Ruth's mother used when she was staying. Some of the things he had bought and left with Ruth lay under a display pillow, and she had also put a small bottle of bootleg liquor there. He emptied the bottle in one drink and had finished the flask that was among the things in his briefcase when he heard a car pulling up.

He heard Ruth putting Lorraine to bed, heard Albert Snyder going into the main bedroom. Some time later, Ruth tiptoed into his hiding place. Whispering, she said that her husband was asleep, asked him if he had found everything, scolded him for being tipsy, and remarked: "Isn't it funny?—One of the men at the party tonight said he would kill Albert if he didn't treat me better." He took off his glasses, put on the rubber gloves, picked up the sash-weight, and, with Ruth following, carrying the other things, walked across the landing. Ruth stood in the doorway to the main bedroom while he was inside, beating her husband to death. Most of the other things were intended toward counterfeiting a burglary. One that was not, a length of cheese-cutting wire, was twisted tight around the dead man's neck, and Judd afterward said: "I have not the slightest recollection of that deed, if I did it, and I would hate to think of placing the blame anywhere, for, God knows, the rest of it was bad enough. I may have done it—Ruth alone can tell. I am willing to accept every bit of the guilt that is mine."

Before leaving her, she on her mother's bed, he bound and gagged her. She had told him to hit her so as to make a bruise that she could blame on "the burglar," but he could not bring himself to do that. More concerned that she might get cold than that the burglary story would seem credible, he started to tuck her imitation-fur coat around her—but she, already re-rehearsing the telling of that story, indicated that he was to throw the coat in a corner. So far as is known, he did not kiss her goodbye.

The sky was lightening when he got back to Jamaica Station, but he was too early for the first train to Manhattan. He took a cab to Grand Central. The driver, dissatisfied with the tip, would remember him— and so, for other reasons, would some of the attendants on the train to Syracuse.

There, he slipped into his hotel (which no longer exists—the Onondaga, it was called) and walked to the floor where his room was. At last he had something to feel grateful for: during the week a school friend living in Syracuse had looked him up, and on the spur of the moment he had concocted a naughty reason for wanting to be surreptitiously away from the hotel on the Saturday night, and the friend had agreed to assist the deception: the DO NOT DISTURB sign over the handle of the door to his room showed that the friend had kept his word. He swallowed a few drinks in his room, then bathed and changed his clothes. Some of those he had been wearing were bloodstained. He stuffed them into a suitcase, which he took with him on the Sunday night when he went to have dinner with his friend—to whom he told more lies, some of them surreal variations on what had really happened in the small house in Queens Village, and who agreed to give further help by arranging for the case and its contents to be destroyed in a furnace. They drank and chatted till late.

Judd had only been back in his hotel room for a few minutes, was starting to undress, when there was a knock on the door. He opened it and did not look surprised—seemed to one of the three men to be glad—when another of them said that they were detectives. He went with them to Syracuse police headquarters. But he refused to believe (desperately needing to *know* that Ruth trusted him, that he could trust her, he did not dare believe) what he was told.

On the Sunday morning—after Lorraine, finding her mother lying bound and gagged, had loosed the kerchief and been sent to fetch help from a neighbor, and after a doctor and detectives had arrived but before the corpse had been removed—Ruth had recited the burglary story. Asked to repeat parts of it, parts that the listening detectives clearly found hard to credit, she had made amendments, and then, getting confused between the original and the revised versions, had become flustered. Meanwhile, investigators had pooh-poohed false semblances of burglary and searched in vain for unequivocal proof of it. When a detective had started reading out men's names in her address book, asking about each of the men, she had looked and sounded frightened as he flicked to the "G" pages and had tried too hard to seem unconcerned when he came to "Judd Gray." She had already been asked about a tie pin with the initials "JG" that had been found on the floor of the main bedroom—and she may have thought that she was telling the truth when she said it was her husband's, a memento of his first love, a girl named Jessie Guishard, who had died while he was engaged to be married to her. The name in the address book, the same initials on the tie pin—the conjunction, exciting the detectives, had set all but one of them ferreting in search of more, and more reliable, information about Judd Gray than the new widow had given, and the detective, who had not let excitement run away with him, had made sure that she knew the purpose of the others' busyness, had waited patiently while she waited with increasing unease, and then had lied to her that Judd Gray had been located and had made a full confession. Instantly falling for the lies because by now she was expecting, dreading, to hear them as gospel truth, she had blurted out that, though she had helped plan the murder, she had played no active part in it and, at the last minute, had tried to dissuade Judd Gray from committing the awful crime.

On the Monday evening, he—still refusing to believe what he had been told over and over, ever more brutally, throughout the day—was taken, handcuffed to one of a scrum of detectives, thrusting through excited crowds, to Syracuse railway station to a reserved carriage of a train to Grand Central. The questioning continued; when one detective needed a rest, another took over. Judd's retorts, never answers, were often flippant, sometimes joking. Dinner was brought in; he insisted on footing the bill. Somewhere near Albany he was shown newspapers, their front pages blackened with headlines announcing Ruth's confession.

And, at last, his resistance began to crack. Detectives from New York City boarded the train. He was asked, "Do you know, Judd, that we have the Pullman ticket that you traveled back on?" Earlier he would have said something of a "so what" sort. He murmured, "Well, gentlemen, I was at the house that night." And from then on he talked and talked—till the train came to a station in Harlem, where the party alighted so as to avoid the mob waiting at Grand Central . . . throughout the car drive to Long Island City . . . in the district attorney's office there—and for two days on the witness stand during the trial, which began less than a month later (the judge who was supposed to preside had been replaced because he "objected to defiling Holy Week with a recital of lust such as that promised by the Snyder-Gray case") and ended a fortnight after Holy Week, with the jury finding both defendants guilty of murder in the first degree.

Any slight chance the woman might have had of gaining a different verdict had been dashed by evidence that she had tricked her husband into signing life-insurance policies, the most beneficial of which,

DAILY ⚫ NEWS

EXTRA EDITION

NEW YORK'S ☞ PICTURE NEWSPAPER

Sunday, 1,357,556
Daily, 1,193,297

Vol. 9. No. 173 56 Pages — New York, Friday, January 13, 1928 — 2 Cents

DEAD!

Story on page 3

(Copyright: 1928: by Pacific and Atlantic photos)

RUTH SNYDER'S DEATH PICTURED!—This is perhaps the most remarkable exclusive picture in the history of criminology. It shows the actual scene in the Sing Sing death house as the lethal current surged through Ruth Snyder's body at 11:06 last night. Her helmeted head is stiffened in death, her face masked and an electrode strapped to her bare right leg. The autopsy table on which her body was removed is beside her. Judd Gray, mumbling a prayer, followed her down the narrow corridor at 11:14. "Father, forgive them, for they don't know what they are doing?" were Ruth's last words. The picture is the first Sing Sing execution picture and the first of a woman's electrocution.—*Story p. 3; other pics. p. 28 and back page.*

basically for $45,000, contained a double-indemnity clause agreeing to double the payout if he died as the result of an accident or in the course of a crime.

The sentences were carried out at Sing Sing during the last few minutes of Thursday, January 12, 1928, only just avoiding Friday the Thirteenth. As soon as Judd Gray's corpse had been carried out of sight, Ruth Snyder was brought into the execution room. Her hair had turned quite gray since the trial, and the henna she had applied to it had produced a muddy yellow, blatantly untrue, not at all attractive. She had decided on and practiced her last words, and when the buckling of the straps was almost done and there was no guard obstructing the view of the witnessing reporters, she spoke the words as if they were original: "Father, forgive them, for they know not what they do." The electricity surged through her body, and a man in the front row of witnesses, among them under the false pretense of being a reporter, clicked a camera he had tied to his ankle.

The picture, fuzzy not only because of the poor illumination but also because of the shuddering convulsions of the subject, filled the front page of the therefore increased number of editions of Friday's *New York Daily News*. Both the taking of the picture and the use of it caused a furor, with the photographer and the *Daily News* editors insisting that they were honorable men who had acted on behalf of posterity—and others, among them some tabloid editors who were just plain jealous, snarling and sneering: "Posterity?—prosperity, doncher mean?" I wonder if any other picture scoop had sold more papers. Although I am sure that the whole enterprise was oh so sleazy, I am just as sure that if I had been in New York on that Friday in 1928, I would have queued for a copy of the *Daily News:* something to do, I suppose, with what Dickens termed "the attraction of repulsion."

I have at home a copy of that *Daily News*—smudged and yellow, rather like Ruth Snyder's final hairdo, and cracking into confetti at the folds. And I have a near-tabloid-size, shocking-pink-colored paperback that was published at twenty-five cents in the summer of 1927. Although both "Own" and "True" are at least overstatements in its title, *Ruth Snyder's Own True Story,* it is said to have so touched or otherwise affected 107 male early readers that they sent her proposals of marriage, should she be reprieved. None of them, nor any of the 164 who proposed after a wistful poem she really had written in the death cell was published, could have been thinking of marrying her for her money, for the Prudential had announced that the policies on her husband's life, null and void from the start, had been made excessively so by the method she had used to reduce the number of premiums.

I also have a book called *Doomed Ship* (a slight borrowing from a poem by Oscar Wilde), which was published posthumously—its author, Judd Gray, having refused to end it till a few hours before his own end. There seems to be no doubt that it is all his own work, and that in itself makes the book almost unique among criminals' autobiographies. The fact that he wrote honestly (which is not to say that everything he wrote was true) makes the book, I think, quite unique. I must remember when I get back to Manhattan to suggest to Hugh Abramson that he should republish it—"restore to print" is the nicely old-fashioned term he prefers.

I have never read James M. Cain's novel *Double Indemnity,* which transforms parts of the Snyder-Gray story as background of a railway-related murder plan, but the movie based on the novel—the screenplay by Raymond Chandler and the director, Billy Wilder—must be the finest film noir that doesn't need English subtitles. Chandler also partly wrote the screenplay of *Strangers on a Train,* and Wilder also partly wrote the script of and directed *Some Like It Hot,* that *perfectly* ridiculous tale that is set in motion, at first on railway lines, by an unintended eavesdropping on an event more than somewhat resembling the St. Valentine's Day Massacre, the real surroundings of which I shall, all being well, be visiting early next week.

Stodgy critics, forgetful of the "Nobody's perfect" tagline of *Some Like It Hot,* have decried Wilder solely on account of the few terrible movies he made—should never have been allowed to make. But I think of his splendid others—more of them, I reckon, than the splendid ones made by any other director, perhaps excepting Frank Capra. One Wilder or one Capra is, for my ticket money, worth a dozen artsy-crafty Ingmar Bergmans, a score of egomaniacal Ken Russells, a whole gross of deceptive Oliver Stones.

We are now some miles, about half an hour's worth, west of Syracuse. Next stop, Rochester, where this Lake Shore Limited will at last start earning its name. Then, after a skirting of one Great Lake, Ontario, arrival at the eastern end of another, Erie: specifically, at Buffalo, where in 1889 William Kemmler murdered his girlfriend, the ornately named Tillie Ziegler, with an ax, consequently becoming the first person to be executed with electricity (so inefficiently that that inaugural occasion very nearly became the last) and where twelve years later Leon Czolgosz shot and fatally wounded William McKinley, subsequently giving no more detailed reason than that, in his anarchic opinion, "the President was the enemy of the good people—the good working people."

I am resigned to *seeing* Buffalo; I shall still be awake, I'm sure. Excepting occasional dots of light and, far less often, nebulous scatterings of them—evidences of tiny, railside towns—the window is black. I know that there is supposed to be only one sort of black; that describing something as rather or very black is considered as much of a nonsense as saying that someone is slightly pregnant—but there *are* sorts of blackness. The window's blackness has been painted on the pane of glass; the dots aren't dots at all but pinpricks.

In Cleveland and Kent

The next thing I know, I have been woken—well, half-woken—by a tapping at the door, which must have ceased a few seconds ago, for Sidney has already slid open the door and unzipped the curtain and is offering me a polystyrene cup of coffee on a floppy cardboard tray, which, because I take it at the opposite-the-cup end, collapses under the weight of the cup, which tips, spilling the coffee on the tray and bed (Sidney doesn't seem upset—or surprised: "That often happens," he says, adding that he'll bring me more coffee, an offer I decline). While he is squeezing the soggy mess of tray into the cup, he is telling me that the time is 6:30, which is when I asked to be called, and that perhaps I ought to hurry as the train will be arriving in Cleveland about twenty minutes earlier than its scheduled arrival time of 7:01.

I feel both peeved (as I hate having to rush at any time, most of all in the early morning) and alarmed because, being so used to British trains, which I have never known to be early, I think that if this Amtrak train can be as much as twenty minutes ahead of when it is meant to get to Cleveland, the driver, clearly not a clock watcher, may give a desultory glance along a deserted trainside at Cleveland and take it into his impatient head that he is free to set off for Sandusky, or wherever the next station is, and I shall still be aboard.

My rushing—to get the bed folded up, to pee, to dress, to wash my face and brush my teeth, to collect my things together—is so effective that I have stopped panting and have almost finished a cigarette when the driver clangs his bell and slows the train into Cleveland Station.

I just hope that Sidney had got it right, that this really is Cleveland Station. I can see no sign proving that it is. (Whereas every station in England, even the smallest, is profuse with such signs, each of Amtrak's seems to have only one, usually tucked behind a Coca-Cola billboard.) Sidney, beside the train, helps me down with my luggage and accepts the accumulated tip of five dollars with (I watch his expression carefully) good grace. I hope that subsequent attendants will be as nice and helpful as he has been.

I see what I take to be a clue that this *is* Cleveland: a woman dressed all in black fustian, including a peasant bonnet, and carrying a basket covered with a black cloth has left the train and walked to the parking lot, where two men, also all in black, wearing hats with low crowns and wide brims, are waiting beside a black surrey (without a fringe on top) that is drawn by a horse that, because it is not black but lint white, is as noticeable as the three people are. They are Shakers: members of an ascetic community, the doctrines of which were formulated in England in the eighteenth century. I know that because once before when I stayed here with the Borowitzes, we went out to lunch on a Sunday to a place close to where the Shakers live and work and afterward bought toffees and pickles, all made from maple fruit, in a shed that the Shaker serving in it politely told me was not, as I had called it, a shop. I know it too because the Borowitzes live in the lovely suburb of Cleveland called Shaker Heights.

The cabbie who drives me to their home does not drive a cab but a minibus. He wears a dilapidated baseball-type cap that says "OK, I admit it—I fought in Vietnam." He knows the way, which makes a pleasant change from the generality of cabbies in New York City (the West Indian one who, after a haggle, agreed to take me from Kennedy Airport to Flushing, accused me of deception when I revealed that I didn't know the route to Flushing either) and which so impresses me that when we arrive I accept his offer to come back in half an hour less than three days' time to return me to the station to catch that day's Lake Shore Limited train, continuing on to Chicago. I hope he feels complimented by my trust, knowing that if I miss that train, I shall be in trouble—for the Lake Shore service, like most of Amtrak's long-distance routes, is rationed to one train a day.

Albert Borowitz is waiting for me by the back porch of the grand house. Everyone who knows him knows him as Al—everyone, that is, except the person who knows him best, his wife, who lives up to her name, Helen, and who keeps his first name intact. He looks like an unusually tall, unusually Jewish leprechaun. He says "Hi!" in that special way of his that I have been looking forward to hearing—a tone that is a mixing of surprise (never mind that one is expected) and delight. Actually, this morning he looks a bit like an ancient Jewish Roman, simply because he is wearing only a bathing toga and sandal-like slippers; the slim-rimmed spectacles near the tip of his nose are immaterial to the impression. It is a bonus to friendship when one admires a friend, and I have several reasons for admiring Al, one being that he is the best of America's crime historians. I am also envious, being a dunce at languages, of his conversance with what seems to be all of them. I gather that his Urdu is a mite rusty.

Although we have not met for almost a year, we chatter, drinking good coffee, as if there had been no break. Helen comes down at a sensible time and joins in the chatter, adding new subjects to it but never once pushing the subject—or subjects—of pictorial art, on which she is an authority; she was for many years a curator at the Cleveland Museum of Art. The treasures and visual pleasures in this house, wonderfully diverse and yet never jarring, one with another, go to show that if a person's taste is fine-tuned, it makes nonsense of interior designers' dogma about which styles and which colors are, as such people insist in their la-di-da way, "conflictive."

Al and Helen go for a dip in the pool, and I go upstairs for a bath—and, meanwhile, to shave (for that is done most efficiently in the bath: the steam opens the pores). And round about noon we leave, Al driving, though Helen is better at it, on the journey across the flatland south of Shaker Heights (I am sometimes reminded of the flatness of East Anglia)—thirty miles or so—to Kent, a small town with a large university. There we go to a house on RocMarie Avenue, so called, I happen to know, because the developer's name was Roc and his wife's Marie—it is as well that their names were not Cy and Phyllis. I have only visited this American Kent a few times before, but I have several friends here. Half a dozen of them are at the house: (1, 2) Dean and Pat Keller, who live in it—he is *a* dean too (of the Kent State University libraries), and I am still unsure what to type on the envelope when I write to him (the longer one has known somebody, the harder it is to ask certain small questions one should have asked at the start); (3, 4) William Hildebrand and his small blond bombshell of a wife, Ann— he, a professor of English at the university, is specially knowledgeable about and devoted to the works of Shelley and Coleridge and (I learned this only recently and, though I knew he had a great interest in true crime, was surprised by it) who first went into book print with a coediting of essays on the death penalty; and (5, 6) a couple, both much younger than the rest of us, Bradley Westbrook and his wife, Barbara, who, though she doesn't look ardently feminist, goes by her maiden name, Bonnice; he is a curator of the special collections in the university libraries.

I don't think Pat Keller is at all Greek, but the meal she cooked certainly was. Made forgetful that I wasn't hungry, I had seconds and was only saved from asking for thirds by recollection of one of my mother's rules of good manners, that one should eat no more than "an elegant sufficiency."

Afterward, and after lots of goodbyes and till-thens, the Borowitzes and I, in their car—which, having been parked out of sight of the sun, has only got to oven-mark 8—follow Dean Keller, in his, on to the campus.

This trip within a trip is at my request. The first time I visited the university, the weather was very different. That was during a weekend of events associated with the opening of the Borowitz True Crime Collection, the culmination of many months of work by members of the library's staff following Al's donation of his extraordinary, also enormous, collection of criminous books, prints, and ephemera. I was here to deliver a dedication lecture at three o'clock on the Sunday, and the night before at the grand dinner an undergraduate student senator had agreed to show Al, his son Peter, and me around a part of the campus.

We met up, I think it was at two. The student was impressively informed and estimably informative, but the trouble was that the temperature was farther below zero than I had ever experienced, and after about half an hour, about halfway through the tour, by which time rigor mortis was already quite advanced in my ears, cheeks, mouth, and nose, my brain started to go numb. I was still able to see, and I found some consolation from seeing that Al and Peter looked as frozen as I was. Having stiffly nodded our thanks to the student (who I'm sure wasn't wearing a jacket, let alone a coat; I was told later that there is something meteorologically odd about Kent, in that it rarely gets more than sixty warm days a year, and so perhaps students' bodies go through an antifreezing evolutionary process), we got to the lecture hall a few minutes before I was due to start talking and while my jaw was still locked. Thank the Lord, there was a slight delay, then William Hildebrand helped by adding some pauses to his introduction of me. Most of me had thawed when my time came—not my nasal passages, though, which meant that every so often my nostrils dripped disconcertingly.

Now on this sweltering hot day Dean Keller is showing Al and me around again. This time Helen is with us—and, sometimes, gangs of black squirrels, prodigiously multiplied from the couple that a groundsman imported here from Canada a long while ago; sitting up, forlornly expectant of our tidbits, they look like charred coffee pots.

That now-retired groundsman is to be thanked or blamed for the extravagance of black squirrels, no doubt about that. And if someone particularly wanted to, he could establish, perhaps to the very day, when the originating couple arrived. Such simple exactnesses are rare. It is usually hard—indeed, often impossible—to tell what sparked a series of incidents. This part of the campus, beside a long gray-stone building, is called Blanket Hill, and what happened here at 12:24 P.M. on Monday, May 4, 1970, was one incident in one of many series of incidents that stemmed from a political decision—what or by whom or when I have no idea, and I doubt if anyone else has—that was taken before the winter of 1961, when President Kennedy decided to send American troops to South Vietnam. On the Thursday before what happened here, President Nixon, himself reacting to one incident in one of many series of incidents, decided that "there is an area . . . immediately above the Parrot's Beak . . . where a combined American and

South Vietnamese operation is necessary." Early the next day, on the grassy Commons that stretch from behind the long gray-stone building, Taylor Hall, the first of many rallies in protest against the "Cambodian Escalation" was held.

The early rallies were peaceful, only of students, but by the evening, following the arrival of what in England we call Rentamobs, they were basically the setting-off points, the sparking-off points, for the infliction of violence and destruction in the town. In the small hours of Saturday, the mayor ordered the closure of all bars (he also imposed a curfew, but no one seems to have been aware of it), and most of the protestors, many of them so drunk that they had forgotten what they were protesting about, straggled back to the Front Campus—where, revived by the sight of policemen, all of them shouted obscenities or threats, and some pelted the policemen with bottles and stones, eventually causing the retaliation of tear gas, which also had a curtailing effect on the confrontation.

From soon after daybreak, while a good many students were helping clear up the town (a task made harder by the clogging of the streets by curious day-trippers, keen to view the damage and hoping to see more damage being done), merchants were warned by protestors that if they did not stick antiwar posters in their windows, their premises would be gutted that night. So many rumors were credited as being news by television and wireless on-the-spot reporters, abiding by the Parkinsonian rule that a story must be expanded so as to fill the time available for its broadcasting, that the local council and university officials got together to set up "rumor-control telephone posts." The mayor announced that the bars were to be closed till further notice and that a curfew would be imposed between dusk and dawn—then, fretting that those precautions were inadequate, he requested help from the Ohio National Guard. Units were dispatched from nearby Akron, where for the past couple of days they had been quelling disturbances by members of the Teamsters Union who, against the wishes of the then-imprisoned owner of the union, James Riddle Hoffa, had come out on strike (shots had been fired at the guardsmen, but none had fired back).

By the time the soldiers arrived in Kent, at nine in the evening, protestors, aided and abetted by fun-loving day-trippers, had vandalized university buildings. Some of them had also thrown incendiary devices into the headquarters of the Reserve Officers Training Corps and then made sure of its complete destruction (it has not been rebuilt) by stoning the firemen and cutting their hoses with machetes. After smaller buildings had been set ablaze, national guardsmen and members of the state's highway patrol began restoring order and were successful by midnight.

On Sunday morning, the governor of Ohio, James Rhodes, arrived in town, apparently with the intention of making things worse. I say apparently because Governor Rhodes, being an intelligent man, accompanied on this occasion by advisers in addition to minders, must have guessed that any inflammatory statements he mouthed into microphones were likely to be overheard. I cannot make out whether or not his voice was in range of any of the microphones when he turned down the county prosecutor's suggestion that the university should be closed for the time being, and so I must stress that he was *quoted* as saying that he, the Honorable James A. Rhodes, was not going to do anything that might be mistaken as kowtowing to groups like the one called Students for a Democratic Society (the first leader of which happened to be a Kent State University dropout). It seems that, till Rhodes had the rush of blood to his vocal chords, members of the university faculty and students respected by their peers were having some success in persuading student-protesters that they had protested too much.

It may be that some of the partial success was lasting—that, but for the pre-Rhodes efforts, more students would have ignored an order banning gatherings and attended a rally on the Commons in the early evening. A number of students obeyed the National Guard commander's order to disperse, but the diminished crowd, heeding other orders, formed a procession toward the town. A phalanx of guardsmen forced them back. By midnight the guardsmen had cleared the Commons; they had used tear gas against the more obstinate protestors. Two guardsmen and two students were in the hospital, none with serious injuries. Sixty-eight persons had been arrested, raising the total since the start of the troubles to 104.

Monday, May 4. Shortly before noon someone began ringing the Victory Bell on the Commons. It is hung within a small oblong of stones, and the whole thing looks to me, standing at the side of Taylor Hall, like one of the communal water wells that, till not long ago, were at the center of many English villages. I have been told that the bell was put up to be rung in celebration of the university's sporting achievements but that it isn't often heard for its intended purpose.

That Monday morning it was rung with the idea of *making* a victory of sorts: rung as a rallying call to students who were willing, or who wanted, to defy the order banning gatherings—to attract them to the tilted area around the Victory Bell, a hundred yards from the ruins of the ROTC building, in front of which were ranks of guardsmen.

The timing was perfect. Fewer than three hundred students came to protest, but there was a half-circling audience of some two thousand, most of them students who, at the noon class break, were in no hurry to get to lunch. The setting was perfect too, a member of the faculty noticed: "The participants [protestors v. guardsmen] faced each other, and the spectators ringed the area—a real Roman circus."

A jeep drove onto the Commons; a campus policeman sat next to the driver, and two guardsmen "rode shotgun" in the back. Of course, a television camera crew followed. Speaking through a megaphone, the policeman said: "This assembly is unlawful. The crowd must disperse. This is an order." He repeated the message four times. It was met with chants of "Pigs off our campus" and, showing some poetical preparation, "One, two, three, four—we don't want your fucking war." Stones were hurled at the jeep. Guardsmen fired tear gas. Fleeing protestors got mixed up with fleeing spectators. Guardsmen, about a hundred of them, wearing gas masks and carrying rifles with bayonets fixed, marched in pursuit.

There are too many disparate accounts of what happened after the guardsmen had passed on either side of the Victory Bell. Anyone still requiring proof that the camera does lie should compare snapshots that clearly were taken at the same moment of the same bit of campus, guardsmen wedging between civilians, and which give contradictory versions of the scene.

Either because of the confusion or by design, the guardsmen were split into two sections. One section, now itself pursued by—flanked by—people shouting at them, pelting them with stones, retreated to the crest of Blanket Hill. There they turned—some dropped to their knees, some of *them,* and perhaps some others, raised their rifles. Most of the rifles were pointed over the heads of the protestors.

The time was 12:24.

Within about as many seconds, thirteen students were dead or were dying or were unfatally wounded. The names of the four students who were dead or dying were Allison Krause, Jeffrey Miller, Sandra Scheuer, and William Schroeder. None of them was closer than thirty yards from the nearest guardsman; two of the wounded students were closer than that.

It seems to me that, if anything is clear about the shootings, it is that one of the guardsmen for some reason, or perhaps without intending to, fired his weapon—and others, exhausted and frightened, involuntarily fired theirs—and others, as exhausted and still more frightened, unreasoningly assumed that they were being fired at, and acted, *re*acted, in self-defense.

If the guardsman who had fired the first shot had a *seen* reason for doing so, it may have been the sight of a man with a pistol running from among the most venturesome students toward the guards' position on the crest of the hill. Moments after the shootings, the man— or *a* man—threatened a group of students with a pistol and, after being chased off by university employees, was disarmed by guardsmen and campus police officers. A freelance press photographer, he claimed that he had brought the weapon with him as a safeguard against damage to himself and his camera from protestors who didn't like having their picture taken. As soon as the weapon had been examined and found to be fully loaded, and the man had produced a permit showing that he was legally entitled to it, he was set free. I must say that I wish the disarmers had concocted an excuse for retaining the weapon and then freed the man in a crowded students' hall; but then I tend to think that, in the matter of criminal acts for which there are no legal punishments, democratic punishments may not be a bad idea.

I have read several accounts of the happenings at Kent in May 1970 and have started to read books about them that turned out to be propaganda. The most objective account I have read—it seems to have emerged from some sort of committee of students and teachers at the university—appeared in the Kent alumni magazine published three months after the events.

Excerpts:

> In the moments following the shootings, the Guard unit reassembled and marched back down Blanket Hill to resume their positions near the remains of the ROTC building.
>
> The frenzied early-afternoon hours brought their share of heroes on campus—those faculty, staff, and students who pleaded and argued with mobs of outraged youngsters bent on "avenging" the shootings right then and there. . . .
>
> In the afternoon, a judge of the Common Pleas Court of Portage County signed an order granting the County Prosecutor's injunction that the university should be closed for several weeks. . . . By nightfall, the campus was devoid of all but a group of 72 international students and residence-hall staff.
>
> It was the beginning of one of the most "unreal" nights the citizens of Kent will ever experience. All traffic in and out of town was halted. Businesses were closed. Military vehicles patrolled the town, and a dusk-to-dawn curfew went into effect. Everyone was off the streets. People clustered on lawns or sat on porches listening to police-band broadcasts. Rumors flew more swiftly than the military helicopters, which circled the town incessantly, shining giant spotlights over houses and yards in an eerie treetop dance.
>
> Kent knew real fear.

> May 5. . . . On this day the campus became headquarters for the world press. . . . At a news conference, the president of the university called for a federal commission to investigate the problems at KSU and said: "I hear lunacy on the one side and frightening repressions on the other, and I don't hear from that traditional center position that says, 'Let us discuss fully and without limits, and let us come to a decision and a conclusion within orderly processes which are in themselves subject to orderly change.'"

> May 6. . . . Six students from the university held a conference of more than an hour with President Nixon at the White House. . . .

May 8. . . . The last National Guard troops left campus in the morning, with the final Highway Patrol officers leaving later in the day. . . . At this point, some 100 FBI agents were conducting the campus and Kent-area investigation. . . .

June 6. . . . One of the last acts of the Ohio state legislature before summer recess was to pass a new campus-riot bill . . . designed to achieve swift action during disturbances. The bill provides strict penalties for outsiders convicted of any of a variety of charges on campuses. The same penalties apply to students and faculty. . . .

June 13. . . . Forty days after their forced exodus from campus, some 1,250 seniors and graduates returned to receive degrees. One of the graduates commented, "This is not only a commencement for us, but for the school too." . . . During the commencement ceremony, a telephone rang on the speakers' platform; the call, it was announced, had come from an Ohio congressman who had received word from the White House that President Nixon had named a special commission to investigate campus unrest. . . .

June 22. . . . The first summer session began, with an enrollment of 7,470, slightly less than the summer enrollment of 7,679 a year ago. "A reasonably normal and complete summer session is presumed," the president of the university said.

It was not till near the end of the 1970s that the last of many legal actions, both criminal and civil, trundled to a conclusion. No national guardsman was found guilty of anything. Compensation was paid to the next of kin of the four dead students and to the nine students who had been injured; the largest amount, $350,000, went to a student whose legs had been paralyzed by a bullet wound in the back.

Something called a Memorial, a scattering of stone slabs and Perspex things like manhole covers near the foot of Blanket Hill, was dedicated on the twentieth 4th of May after the shootings. It doesn't appear to my eyes to have the slightest significance, but I suppose that is why the committee appointed to choose from among dozens of submitted designs chose this one: being visually meaningless, it cannot

Dean Keller (left) and Albert and Helen Borowitz at the May 4 Memorial, Kent State University, Kent, Ohio.

offend anyone except for that reason; it is otherwise uncontroversial. I am glad that a small white stone of remembrance, shaded by a tree that can have been no more than a cutting when the stone was placed, has not been removed.

The first time I stayed with the Borowitzes, in 1987, I was kept as happily busy as I am this time. It was through a weekend when a theater festival partly sponsored by the Borowitzes was occupying all three of the refurbished theaters in what is now called Playhouse Square. Having no idea that any of the events would be posh, I had not thought to bring my dinner jacket. When we got ready to go to the first of them, Al put on a lounge suit, as I had, and Helen put on a knee-length frock—and it turned out that we were the only ones at the very grand event who were not dressed to the nines. I was too grateful to them for saving me from singular embarrassment to tell them that I was grateful.

Much of the festival was a tribute to that extraordinary man of the theater, George Abbott, who was about to be one hundred years old. He was there, and I told him, probably reminded him, that when the great jazz pianist Eubie Blake reached a hundred, he remarked, "If I'd known I was going to live this long, I would have taken better care of myself." (As is to be expected, Mr. Abbott has died since then—a fact that makes me think of a story, perhaps made up, about that earlier great showman P. T. Barnum, who, hearing of the death of his star turn, the Human Cannonball, moaned, "It will be hard to find another man of his caliber." I hope that an author who cherishes the theater, and must therefore be thankful to Mr. Abbott, is unhurriedly writing his biography—at least two volumes of it, surely, because even before his life was half over, he had done an amazing number of different theatrical things, some of them important, and had done most of them well. Although there cannot be many people with reliable memories left alive who saw him playing young parts created by other writers and directors, those performances can be brought flickeringly to mind from faded clippings. But as for his other work, so much of it—as a collaborating writer [for instance, with Rodgers and Hart on *The Boys from Syracuse* and *On Your Toes,* and with respective others on, among dozens of hits, *Damn Yankees, The Pajama Game,* and *Fiorello!*] and as director or producer, or both, of some of those shows and many others, ranging from the dark *Pal Joey* to the effervescent *Call Me Madam*—that work remains—will remain—as part of a bountiful treasure for all of us.)

This time with Al and Helen: following the trip to Kent, they take me to Lake View Cemetery and into the towered monument, flagrant and yet somehow cozy, to James Garfield, one of the remarkable number of presidents born in Ohio, who was fatally shot by Charles Guiteau, a paranoid swindler and fringe religionist, while Garfield was walking to board a train at the Baltimore and Potomac Depot in Washington, D.C., in July 1881. The monument was designed by George Keller. I wonder whether Keller is a common American name, tell myself that I must remember to ask Dean Keller if he is descended from George, and of course forget to when I see him at a lunch of the NOBS, the Northern Ohio Bibliophilic Society, for which Al and I pay our way by afterward talking to them, by turns taking unexpected cues from each other, about "Our Lives in Crime."

One night we dine at home (starting with New England clam chowder, which Helen knows I'm partial to); on another at a fish-specializing restaurant called the Watermark, which is in the Flats beside the Cuyahoga River, an erstwhile manufacturing area of Cleveland that, rather like St. Catherine's Dock in London, has been "rejuvenated" (the meal, excellent anyway, is enhanced since Al has arranged for us to be at a brolly-topped table on the verandah—as the twilight darkens, the thousands of different-colored reflections on the river become as bright as, then brighter than, the lights that make them, and I become less tetchy about a pleasure boat that keeps traveling back and forth between turning points that cannot be more than a furlong apart, blaring rap music that has made me think of the line in *Private Lives* about an orchestra with a remarkably small repertoire). And on another night, after window-shopping around the galleries of Tower City, risen from where Cleveland's railway station used to be, we eat at the Stage Deli in the basement. (I suppose that this Stage Deli is an offshoot of that always-packed one in Manhattan, where John Lennon ate before going home to the Dakota apartment block where Mark Chapman, who seems to have had either too much love for the songs of the sort that Lennon had stopped writing or excessive hatred of the record-track fillers that he had turned to, was waiting to shoot him to death.)

One morning, we drive the forty or so miles southwest to Medina (which, pronounced Med*i*na here, would certainly be Med*ee*na in England) and look at the toy-town square—look longest at the pretty, red-brick county courthouse where, in 1925, Martha Wise, an agricultural spinster who was suspected by some of being a witch, was found guilty of murdering three relatives with household poison for motives that remain obscure and sentenced to life imprisonment—and then visit a "collectibles market" in the largest community hall I have ever seen. Helen buys quaint buttons and beads; Al buys lots of odds and ends, including a shiny campaign badge that says ELIOT NESS FOR MAYOR OF CLEVELAND; and I, constrained by the need to keep my luggage light, buy just one thing: a pristine copy of the *Cleveland Press* of July 17, 1915, with a top-of-the-front-page illustrated report that a New York jury, the best that money could buy, had decided that crazy Harry Thaw, the murderer of Stanford White, was as sane as they were and thus (I have never understood the legal logic of this) could be freed rather than transferred from an asylum to a prison.

And on another morning, Al and I, leaving Helen at home, drive to the skyscraping headquarters of the law firm of which he is a partner. The building, which looms over Lake Erie, must have as many suites of offices as a London Inn of Court has chambers. Al puts his car in the high-security parking dungeon, and we go up in a lift to the main entrance and walk out into the courtyard, in the center of which is a statuary jazz band.

We are a few minutes early for our rendezvous with Detective Nate Sowa, an enthusiastic member of the Cleveland Police Historical Society. I suggest to Al that "Nate" is short for Nathan, and he says that it may be a more considerable shortening of Nathaniel; but when Nate arrives, exactly on time in a white police car, he tells us sheepishly, when asked, that he was baptized Ignatius. He doesn't look like a policeman: he is slightly built; wears spectacles; has black hair, receded from his forehead but verdant above his lips; smokes cigars; and is, I guess, in his thirties.

On our way to where we are going he tells us, again when asked, that he specializes in "deterring and apprehending car thieves—a forty-eight-hour-a-day job, because Cleveland is the car-theft capital of the world." As we pass through an area that was once filled with factories but is now one immense parking lot, he refers to it as "a smorgasbord for the auto bangers," adding, "They aim for the 'sweet spot'—and, zip, thirty seconds later, they're in the next county." The "sweet spot," he explains, is the place on a car window where the makers of the safety glass advertise themselves in little gray letters; the imprinting of the letters has the effect of making that inch of the window less safe, and a car thief usually only has to stab the ad once with a screwdriver to make the window disintegrate. Nate nods agreement with my comment that Lewis Carroll would have approved of advertising that invalidates what it advertises—and smiles (he is a most affable man) when Al expresses the hope that there is no advertising copy on condoms.

Before Nate picked us up, Al told me a few things about the man Nate has arranged for us to meet, one being that his name is Gus Zukie, and, anticipating my questions, said that "Gus" was a shortening of "Gustave" and that "Zukie" was a shortening of a tongue twister that probably ended with "ovitch." Wrong again. Once we are settled in a suburban restaurant called Gene's Place, Gus tells me that he was baptized Auguste (that was well over three quarters of a century ago) and that his father, a Russian immigrant, added "ie" to his abrupt surname, thinking that the addition would make it sound more American. Gus is a chunky old gentleman who keeps his white golfer's cap on at the table. He was a Cleveland police constable from the mid-1930s. Nate, sitting next to him, leans to hear what he says and agrees—enthusiastically but deferentially—with most of his ideas for improving police efficiency. And he grins hugely when Gus, complaining that "anyone can get into the police force these days," refers to a newly recruited officer who is supposed to have said, "Last week I couldn't spell 'police'—but now I is one."

The walls of Gene's Place are barely visible between hundreds of glossy photographs of people who were famous in the 1930s, '40s, and '50s, and items on the menu are named in remembrance. Al has a Joan Crawford, which includes ham and hard-boiled eggs; Nate has a Jean Harlow, described as "a petite tenderloin"; Gus, who is on a diet, has a Gypsy Rose Lee, "a real waist-watcher's paradise"; and I, feeling obliged to, have a John Dillinger, which is "smuggled onions and swiped Swiss cheese on grilled rye." My appetite whetted by that, I look forward to an anonymous apple dumpling; but as none of the others wants afters, I say that I don't want any either.

With Gus in the front passenger seat, we drive back to midtown Cleveland to Kingsbury Run, a wide and sometimes deep ravine that, starting from the direction of Shaker Heights, twists and turns through the city till it can slice no farther, having reached the estuary of the Cuyahoga, close to the Flats. It is more desolate now than it was in the 1930s. Then it was busy with freight trains, day and night. The rails are still here, but only a couple of sets, those on which the local rapid-transit trains run, have kept their shine, are not hemmed with grass and weeds. The black signal gantries straddling the Run are mottled with rust, some of it as bright red as the flowers of some of the weeds.

Gus was born and brought up in one of the tiny single-story houses in the clearings on this western side, and he spent a lot of time patrolling the Run when he was a rookie policeman. Although, as I gather, he has rarely returned since then, he usually knows exactly where we are. As Nate drives between the trees, sometimes bumpity-bump on negligible tracks or no track at all, Gus murmurs directions or warnings: "Take a right. . . . Take a left. . . . Careful at this bend, it comes back on itself." Then: "OK, park somewhere along this embankment." And we get out.

There are some old wooden cottages—shacks—beside the road that runs along the embankment. Most of them are still homes. By the sound of it, all of the residents are addicted to television, and each is presently watching a different channel. The occupied cottages look as uninhabitable as the empty ones, but most of them are freshly painted in colors—several colors per cottage—that are all unorthodox for outside decoration, and there are flowers that have been tended in the patches of earth around them. The resident of the nearest cottage must have the use of a lawnmower, for the oblong of grass opposite, on the embankment side of the road, has recently been mowed, making it look like an extension to the paltry property. I glance at Al and can tell that he is as agreeably saddened as I am by the effort to improve the view from the front windows. (I believe that Victor Hugo got it right when he said that "melancholy is the pleasure of being sad.")

Gus skirts the oblong of cut grass (the scent from it is so high pitched that, after a single deep breath, one cannot smell it) and saunters to the edge of the embankment. "Come on," he says, and we do. He points to one of the shelves of the embankment. "Near that straggle of ferns," he says. "See it? That's where the first two were found."

They were found by some boys who had been playing on the slope. It was Monday, September 23, 1935. They lay a yard or so apart—supine, arms by their sides, heels together. One was completely naked; the other was naked except for socks. The skin of the body of the older man was not unlike that of a wind-fallen russet apple that no one has bothered to pick up. (That was not because the body had lain in the open for long: according to doctors, neither of the men had been dead for more than about a week, and the absence of blood on the ground, though both men were decapitated and emasculated, indicated that they had died or been killed elsewhere and their incomplete bodies brought to this place; a scientist hazarded the guess that the "leathering" and discoloring of the skin of the body of the older man was due to "the application of some unknown [perhaps preservative] chemical.")

Policemen who searched this stretch of Kingsbury Run found all sorts of perplexing objects, some of which may have been associated with the crimes—but the only things certainly associated were the two heads, which were planted, so to say, in soft earth, and, near where the heads were unearthed but in plain sight, the genitalia. The identity of

Kingsbury Run, Cleveland, Ohio.

the younger man was established by the matching of his fingerprints with those of a petty criminal that were filed at police headquarters; questioning persons still living in the seedy part of Cleveland where he had lived, sometimes sleeping rough (very rough at times, according to one story—in graveyards or beside the tracks in Kingsbury Run), revealed that he was indiscriminate with regard to sexual partners and suggested that he was bisexual. Thinking that the older man may have

Gus Zukie, puzzled for a moment as to the location of one of the murder sites in Kingsbury Run.

been a hobo, the police quizzed the hundreds of them encamped along the sides of parts of Kingsbury Run. Neither those efforts nor many others produced the slightest apparent clue: the police were unable to identify him, could not even find anyone who said they thought they remembered seeing a man with a face like the dead one on the photograph they were shown. (I wonder whether any effort was made to confirm or contradict the scientist's guess about the use of "some unknown . . . chemical," which, if correct, might have indicated the murderer's occupation or avocation.)

Usually unerringly, Gus leads us—or rather leads Nate, who drives as if he and the car are a single machine—to areas where other corpses subsequently turned up, all but a couple of far-flung ones in or close to Kingsbury Run. (As with the crimes in Whitechapel, London, circa 1888, that are ascribed to "Jack the Ripper," I still need to be convinced that the crimes credited to the "Mad Butcher of Kingsbury Run" were all his own work—that none was a copycat killing by someone, envious or opportunistic, who had decided to get in on his act.) The third was the body of a woman; parts were found in one place, most of the rest, though never the head, in another. The body was identified, from fingerprints, as that of a prostitute who had preferred a number of aliases to her real name, which was Florence Polillo.

In December 1935, a month before portions of the late Florence Polillo first came to light, the newly elected mayor of Cleveland had recruited a former agent of the Treasury Department's Prohibition Bureau as the city's director of public safety, responsible for crime prevention, traffic control, and firefighting. The new director's name was Eliot Ness. Between 1929 and 1932 he had made that name famous by publicizing and encouraging journalists to publicize his leadership of a Chicago-based task-force of "bootleg busters" who—never mind that their successes were more showy than significant—were said to be remarkably honest, fully deserving their press-invented title, "The Untouchables."

The Eliot Ness legend, still flourishing, indeed dilating (more and more people seem to have been misled into unswervable belief that he did something or other toward putting Al Capone in prison), has foundations that are only slightly less flimsy than those of the legend associated with the namesake loch in Scotland.

The appointment of Ness, still only thirty-two, as Cleveland's protector was made on grounds that had more to do with public relations than with public safety: understandably, I suppose, considering that administrators and businessmen needed glossing of the city's image prior to events that, all being well, would attract millions of visitors with billions of dollars—in June the Republican National Convention and the opening of the Great Lakes Exposition, a kind of world's fair that was intended to run for the rest of the summer and to reopen at the start of the next; in September, the American Legion's convention.

Al asks Gus if he saw anything of Ness. "Oh, sure," Gus says, "I admired his dress-sense," and adds, pleasingly to me, "He was a guy you had to be impressed with, even after you saw through the impression." By now, we are on the riverfront, shadowed by a gigantic turntable bridge that has not turned for years. The debris of the dead docks, close to the end of Kingsbury Run, makes this area like a scrapyard seen through a magnifying glass.

Nate Sowa (left) and Albert Borowitz stand beside the Cuyahoga River, with Cleveland's skyline in the background. The three tallest buildings are, from the left, the Society National Building (Cleveland's newest skyscraper), the BP Building, and Terminal Tower (rising above Tower City).

If I have not lost count, we are about halfway between where bodies eight and nine were found. There were, it is generally reckoned, three to go. The last two—one of a man, the other of a woman—were found on August 16, 1938; they were lying close together on a dump, but it appeared, from their respective states of decomposition, that they had been discarded at different times. Like eight of the previous ten, they were never identified.

Nor was the Mad Butcher.

It is easy to say that the police should have done this, should have done that; but one cannot help thinking, after scanning some of the per-body accumulations of possible, probable, or undoubtable clues, that if only someone more sensible than Eliot Ness had been in charge—someone who, understanding that there can be a great difference between facts and information (not all facts are informative), had tipped the contents of all the per-body files into a bin, put a gang of astute sorters to work on the reports, and, when the bin was empty, deputed just one detective, a man who had not been involved with any of the cases and was therefore more likely to see the wood for the trees, to seek connections between categories that the sorters had considered unconnected—then the police, not the murderer, would have ended the killings of persons no one mourned, no one missed.

Gus nods in such a devious way that I don't know if he is agreeing with or humoring me. We are driving back to Al's office building, and, as I am sitting behind the driver's seat, I cannot see Nate's face, the expression on it.

I mention to nobody in particular that the Kingsbury Run story interests me only because it is an unsolved case of serial killing—and then, gathering from the perplexed frown on Al's face that I haven't put enough stress on "unsolved," add that solved cases of serial killing bore me because the caught culprits are invariably boring individuals, made to seem still more boring by the jargon-infested analyses of them that are spouted by psychiatrists. It seems to me, I say (trying not to sound like a psychiatrist myself), that serial killers have one other thing in common: I cannot think of an exception to the rule that they are, by definition, boring—and that it is the boring nature of them, the fact that they are nonentities, that urges them to kill: to try to prove to themselves as much as to the editor of *The Guinness Book of Records* that they are of some importance and power, persons to be reckoned with, worthy of public notice.

I wouldn't cite serial killers' justifiable lack of self-esteem as a reason for pooh-poohing the dozens of crackpot notions that Jack the Ripper was a person of consequence—a brilliant surgeon, a prominent politician, or the Queen of Romania—but only because there are so many other reasons for condemning each of those notions, one being that none of them is supported by the tiniest mite of evidence that would stand up in court. The spouters of who-Jack-was notions, needing to be equally dogmatic about who he wasn't, are unanimously opposed to the candidacy of the least unlikely of the named "suspects"—George Chapman, who was hanged in 1903 for the murder of one of the three women he had poisoned to death at his pub near Whitechapel. They expel him from consideration simply because, so they insist, murderers never, but never, use more than one method for more than one murder. The "never" is one of their countless nonsenses. When I get to San Francisco, I shall be visiting the vicinity of the two murders by a single person in the Emmanuel Baptist Church—one victim cut to death, the other, killed at much the same time, strangled. If the term *piffle-ology* were not such a lumpy mouthful, I should campaign for its replacement of "Ripperology."

Perhaps not intentionally Gus changes the subject—from the killing of a half-dozen whores in the slummy East End of London to the close shaves of a larger number within a police precinct of Cleveland.

He tells us the story of Charles the Clipper, which happened before he retired. An arrested prostitute needed a bath, and it was then noticed that her pubic hairs were crew cut. Initially tight-lipped regarding the bristle, she eventually revealed that a few nights before, having been hired by a nicely spoken, well-dressed man, she had glanced up after dropping her knickers and lifting her skirt and noticed that the customer, still entirely well dressed, had taken a cutthroat razor from one of his pockets. Her fright turned to perplexity when he also produced a battery-powered pair of clippers, a tube of shaving cream, a white napkin, and a can of talc. He explained that he derived exquisite pleasure from shaving female pubic areas, and she—thinking, "Oh well, *à chacun son goût*," or English words to that effect—allowed him to enjoy himself. When he was quite clearly quite satisfied, he pocketed the shaving things, paid her (adding a tip), and departed.

She told the inquisitive policewoman that she had not seen the man before or since, but that in chatting about him to others of her calling, she had learned that he was a frequent shaver. The police, concerned that he might turn into a Sweeney Todd, questioned local prostitutes, but none admitted having been shaved, and some got quite haughty, saying that it was a disgrace to suggest that they would permit the private parts of their bodies to be used for such a purpose.

Gus came up with a way of spotting prostitutes who had recently had close encounters with Charles the Clipper, as the man had been dubbed in police circles. It was to watch out for those who, between customers, were scratching anywhere near their crotches. When they were examined at the station, most proved to have a five o'clock shadow, made itchy by contact with, for instance, nylon, and some of them were persuaded to help the police with their inquiries—which were therefore soon successful, revealing the Clipper as a university professor of a Romance language.

There was no apparent crime to charge him with, and so he was politely warned that if he was ever apprehended and found to be carrying concealed shaving things, hair-raising tales about his extramural activities would be leaked to the president of the university. A marked reduction in the number of visibly itchy prostitutes indicated that the warning had had its intended effect.

Al and I say goodbye to Gus, who, refusing to look tired, doesn't get out of the car, and to Nate, who is going to drive him home. I say, meaning it, that I hope to meet them again the next time I come to Cleveland.

To Chicago

As I got up even earlier this morning than he did on the morning I arrived. He woke me, put the coffee on, and made sure that I hadn't gone back to sleep; and I had time for two cups of coffee (the second with a sleepy Helen too), though the cab driver of a minibus arrived twenty minutes before he was supposed to. All being well, I shall see the Borowitzes next month, for they are leaving soon on one of their at-least-annual trips to England, and I should be back home before their last weekend there.

The cabbie told me, as if saying something I should be grateful for, that temperatures in Cleveland during the past few days were the highest ever recorded for this time of the year. As soon as I get to the Knickerbocker Hotel, which is where I'm staying in Chicago, I must ask for my sweaty shirts to be laundered. The cabbie got me to the station a quarter of an hour before the Lake Shore Limited train was supposed to leave—half an hour before it actually did.

I am not in a sleeper, of course; the ETA at Chicago is 1:03 this afternoon. The seats in these ordinary carriages are not uncomfortable. They are in pairs each side of the aisle. They have folding footrests. The old lady sitting next to me, by the window (she is knitting, I cannot imagine what, for it seems to have at least a dozen short arms—a cozy for a hat stand, perhaps?), is so small that her feet dangle some inches above the footrest. Smoking isn't allowed here, only in the sleepers and in the café—and only in a four-table area there.

The first time I went to the café, I sat facing a man and a woman, both in their thirties and plump, who were drinking beer from cans. Both were wearing baseball-type caps (his in support of a football team, hers advertising a supermarket) and white T-shirts (his remarkably blank, hers printed with quotations from the Bible). He was dark haired, and she was blond.

After eavesdropping on what they were saying, I apologized for doing so and asked if they would mind repeating things into my little tape recorder, which I had taken from my pocket. He, saying nothing, looked doubtful; but she said to him, "Aw, come on, Wayne. This gentleman is from Great Britain. I can tell," and then asked me, "Am I correct, sir?" and then said to him, "There. The Great British are our friends. They helped us with that horrid old Arab guy with the big moustache in Iran or Iraq or wherever the hell it was. Don't be so almighty suspicious—I've chided you about that before, remember?"

He said, "Tricia."

"Well?"

"If I'm gonna talk into that machine, you've got to keep quiet for up to but not exceeding five seconds. Think you can manage that?"

"Ain't he a hoot?" she asked me.

Before I could decide whether to say yes (perhaps offending him, for it is not everyone who likes being described as a hoot) or no (perhaps offending him, for he may have taken a certain arcane pride in being thus described) he told her, "Your first five seconds are up," then asked me what I wanted to know.

I asked about a place they had both pronounced, using a capital H, as the "Holler," but which I had gathered was spelt "Hollow."

Edited extracts from the tape recording:

He: It's just that we've been visiting, Tricia for the first time, with an uncle who lives ten miles from [*location deleted; it is in central Ohio*], and I guess you might say she's been given an education in making and hiding moonshine, which is what illegal liquor is called.

She: And Wayne's Uncle Bill, he took us back to the Hollow. Know what a Hollow is? Me neither till Uncle Bill showed us his. It's at the lowest part of the hill across from his home—it goes down, a kind of tunnel, one way in, another way out—a place for making moonshine. Wayne's family, this particular branch of it, has lived in them parts for—well, a hell of a long time, right, Wayne? Well, see, they've always made their own pottery to keep their moonshine in. The pottery—it's a family brand—distinctive. Different moonshiners make their pottery different ways. And they hide these jars they keep the moonshine in. Have to, you see, because the government don't approve of moonshine because they don't make any tax money out of it. Uncle Bill carries on the family tradition. You should just see where he lives: it's just gorgeous, no other word—these crazy old buildings just as they always were, except some of them lean over enough to alarm you. And all the animals just run free as birds.

He: There's a shaggy horse, twenty-one years old—looks like a burro.

She: Like a mule is what Wayne means to say. And there's a sheep that looks like it's a hundred and fifty years old, and it's the biggest old sheep I've ever seen.

He: Looks like a horse—like a *big* horse.

She: Biggest old horse I've ever seen.

He: When you get near Uncle Bill's place, probably about fifteen dogs meet you, and they ain't necessarily friendly.

She: The folks around there, they'll shoot you if they don't like the look of you. Uncle Bill told of how, when the Revenuers are coming, the local cops let him know before, so he can hide the moonshine. That's because the local police chief has a taste for Uncle Bill's mixture. One time when the Revenuers were coming, the cops didn't know until the last minute, so they helped him dig a big hole where the potatoes were—dug the moonshine down in the ground, then put the potatoes back on top. And he told me the Revenuers stood within inches of it, and they were saying, "we know there's 'shine around here somewhere—there's just got to be 'shine around here," and he just whistled a tune of his own composition.

He: The Revenue planes can go over and detect it. There's a sensor in the planes, see? They fly through, real low, and if they sense it, they know, the bastards, they know.

She: We went up to the Hollow in Uncle Bill's five sisters' car. He was with us because, if he hadn't been with us, the dogs wouldn't have let us in. The sisters, they all live near where his land starts, and Uncle Bill, he told me: "If you hadn't been with Wayne, who the sisters know, they would have come out and peppered your arse" (scuse me for quoting) "with buckshot." They shot one guy they didn't recognize—he was a relative—shot him right through the bottom of the belly, damn near ruining his prospects, if you get my drift. Those sisters, they're very backward. They go to work someplace else, and they come home, and that's the story of their life, right?

He: Same with Uncle Bill. He's fifty years old, and he comes out to get gas and stuff, and that's all. He don't want civilization. There ought to be more people like that. Everyone wants civilization— but if you ask me, civilization ain't all it cracked up to be.

She: Aw, give over, Wayne—Denver ain't so bad. That's where we live. We can't be away too long because of the pets.

He: Snakes.

She: Eleven snakes—eel*ev*'n, would you believe?

He: Big snakes.

She: Real big ones.

He: Six and eight footers. They're re-tic-u-lators.

She: That means they squeeze things.

He: Yeah—like I was endeavoring to say, they squeeze things. That's where they get the name re-tic-u-lators from. They constrict, like boa constrictors—constrict means the same as retict. When you inhale, they tighten.

She: "They curl round their prey" is how I've heard it described.

He: But me, I hang them around my neck. They don't hurt me. But I make damned sure I don't breath in, man.

She: Damned sure. But don't misunderstand: they're tame—tame like any other pets.

He: Two years ago—

She: Just like dogs or cats or—

He: Two years ago, when I got amiable with Tricia, she said, "If you bring those sons of bitches into the house, I'm moving." Now she's got her own personal ones. They grow on you.

She: Yeah, now I've got my own. We bred two of them last year. I can see you're wondering how. For decency's sake, don't ask. But we made $3,000. No exaggeration. We have another pair that's breeding right now. When we're going to be away, like now, we take them, just like dogs, to a boarding kennel. Costs about a hundred dollars a snake, but that ain't unreasonable: they're monstrous eaters—rats and rabbits for preference. So we raise our own vermin as foodstuff.

He: I asked Uncle Bill if he'd like a re-tic-u-lator . . .

She: As a gift, you understand. Wayne's generous.

He: . . . but he declined. Maybe he didn't understand the meaning of the word *re-tic-u-lator.*

By the time I got back to my seat, the very little old lady had started knitting yet another arm. It occurred to me that if she were to lengthen the dozen of them by a couple of yards, Wayne and Tricia might be interested in buying the result as a sleeping bag for their reticulators, each sleeping singly but with their heads or tails sociable in the middle. For fear of dozing and having a snaky nightmare, I tried to put snakes and knitwear out of my mind and to resist drowsiness by reading the paper, the *Plain Dealer,* I had bought at Cleveland Station.

I had almost finished it when I first noticed the elderly man with a white flower in his buttonhole. I noticed him only because he was taking notice of *me.* On his way along the aisle, I supposed to the lavatory, he had slowed down so as to give himself more time to peer. He went past, and a few minutes later I became aware that he, I supposed on his way back from the lavatory, had stopped to look down at, to examine, me. I energetically shook the newspaper, intending that as a sign that I was uncomfortable under his scrutiny, and he explained: "I much admire your jacket, sir." He was smiling admiringly. I am never sure how to respond to a vicarious compliment. This time, I murmured thanks on behalf of the jacket. He continued his return journey along the aisle.

But soon he was back again. "I have spoken to my wife," he said, "and she told me you wouldn't mind if I asked." He hesitated, then asked: "Would you consider selling your jacket?" I must say that I was surprised—partly because there is nothing special about the jacket, which didn't cost very much; partly because it is at least ten years old; and partly, chiefly, because I had never expected to be asked such a question about anything I was wearing. I decided that I must be firm, else he might give up on the jacket and start taking a fancy to my moleskin trousers, and so I said, "No," and immediately pretended to be rereading the *Plain Dealer*.

He muttered something, whether sad or apologetic I couldn't make out, and went away, and when I was sure he was not coming back, I gave myself a part in a Hitchcock movie: there was more to my jacket than had met my eyes, the man with the flower in his buttonhole was Claude Rains, covetous of the CIA microfilm that Madeleine Carroll had sewn in the lining, and at any minute Peter Lorre, so competitively covetous that he had just killed Claude Rains in the lavatory, would appear by my side and threaten to kill me too if I didn't hand over my jacket. The microfilm reason for wanting such a shabby, unspecial garment seemed more likely than admiration of it.

Places along the way:

Elyria (twenty-five miles west of Cleveland). I said to the knitting lady: "What shall I do in Elyria? My brother he is in Elysium," but she either didn't appreciate the almost-Shakespearean joke or was upset because I had made her drop a stitch.

Bryan (thirty-five miles west of Elyria). I learned from the Amtrak route guide, a folder available to all passengers, that this town is "the home of the Spangler Company, makers of DumDum Lollipops and Double Bubble Gum"—also that, as Bryan is on the border between Eastern and Central Times, I had to set my watch back an hour. It is said that Mabel Normand, the silent-movie star who may have murdered the director William Desmond Tayler, couldn't be bothered to keep setting her watch backward or forward when traveling between time zones and therefore carried a collection of watches with different settings, replacing one with another as she traveled, throwing away those that were no longer correct.

South Bend (a hundred miles west of Bryan). I saw tokens—the most spectacular, a gold dome glistering in the sunlight—of the University of Notre Dame. I should feel ashamed that all I know about the university is that it has, or has had, a renowned football team and that "Dame" is pronounced as if it were English. One of the nastiest stories I know is of a Parisian who, trying to commit suicide by jumping from a high part of Notre Dame Cathedral, landed on a flower barrow and its owner, killing her, and, himself unscathed, lived happily ever after. Unusual proof of the definition of suicide as a permanent solution to a temporary problem.

Gary, Indiana (twenty-five miles southeast of Chicago). To my mind's ear, the name of this steel town and the name of the state are inseparable, simply because they are repeated, always together, over and over again, in the lyric of the lisping boy's song in *The Music Man,* which is one of my favorite shows. The train was half an hour late here . . .

. . . and because of what a voice on the loudspeaker called "pre-terminus safety stops"—three of them, each of at least ten minutes—it was well past two o'clock when the train dawdled into Union Station, Chicago.

The Knickerbocker is the sort of hotel that Americans who have not stayed at many English hotels would probably think of as being a very English sort of hotel. Marble floors, acres of polished wood, judiciously few chandeliers, lots of leather armchairs. The main restaurant, which is called the Prince of Wales, used to be an officers' club, and the bar, which is called the Limehouse Pub, is decorated and furnished in much the same way as I imagine the officers' club was. All of the visible employees are dressed in black, with spotless white linen and just-brushed shoes, and some of the men wear frock coats. My only complaint about my room (which has a pleasant view, partly of Lake Michigan) is that a copy of Constable's *Hay Wain* on the wall facing the bed is in Technicolor; as I am sure that it glows in the dark, tonight I shall drape a bath towel over it before trying to get to sleep.

The cabbie who brought me here from the station agreed to come back at three to drive me around town, to some buildings and a blank space I want to look at. It is only five-to when I return to the entrance hall, and so I wander away through passages—and happen upon a lovely little baroque theater, all gilt and gingerbread, *within the hotel.* Perhaps it has never been used as a theater—only for conferences and, with the rows of seats removed, dances—but a theater is what it is: one seemingly bespoke to Restoration comedies (no tragedy could be taken seriously in such frivolous surroundings). If it were in, say, Salzburg or, I must admit, Cheltenham, the local tourist board would advertise it high on the list of Sights to See.

The cabbie, waiting when I come out of the Knickerbocker, is a large black man wearing a tweed cap and a rusty black suit. He looks startled but says, "OK by me, sir," when I ask if I may sit next to him. His Christian name, I see from his identification card on the dashboard, is Hurshell. As I have guessed that he is in his sixties, I am surprised when, after we have been driving for a while and chatting for a shorter time, he says that he aims to retire next year on the day before his eightieth birthday. He was a soldier toward the end of the Second World War, stationed for a few months in England, and he is careful not to appear proud that he took part in the D-Day landings. He is blatantly proud of his son, who is a Baptist minister.

Our first stop is on the South Side, in the district called Kenwood. As I get out, Hurshell cautions me to stay within his sight. "I don't know if the term is familiar to you, sir, but this is what we describe as a ghetto area—not a nice neighborhood."

It used to be. In 1924 it was one of the wealthiest parts of Chicago. The Franks family lived at 5052 Ellis Avenue. A corner house, not quite a mansion, the timber facings still painted white, it is now a nursery school; part of the garden, not quite grounds, is segregated from the street by a tall wire fence, indicating that it is the school's playground. The Loeb family lived along the block, at 5017 Ellis Avenue; I know that that building, truly a mansion, was demolished well over a quarter of a century ago. I know too that another mansion, number 4754 on nearby Greenwood Avenue, which was the Leopold family's home, was demolished longer ago.

In the late afternoon of Wednesday, May 21, 1924, Nathan "Babe" Leopold, who was nineteen, and his homosexual friend Richard Loeb, who was a year younger, abducted fourteen-year-old Robert Franks, a distant cousin of Loeb's, while he was walking down Ellis Avenue from his school toward his home, smashed his skull with a chisel, drove with

5052 Ellis Avenue, Chicago, once the Franks family home.

the body to marshland beside the tracks of the Pennsylvania Railroad, and after submerging the face in water to ensure death and pouring acid on it in the hope of hindering identification, stuffed the corpse down a large drainpipe. Both Leopold and Loeb were reckoned to be geniuses, and it seems probable that they committed the murder, not their first crime in partnership, to prove to themselves how jolly clever they were. But their "perfect murder" was so imperfectly planned and carried out that even the local police, a ragtag force in those days, were able to put clue and clue together to make an ironclad case against them.

Their lives were saved through the rhetorical efforts of Clarence Darrow, the defense lawyer who achieved as many miscarriages of justice in America during the first thirty years of the twentieth century as did Edward Marshall Hall in England over about the same period. Leopold and Loeb—dubbed "the thrill killers" by the tabloids—were sentenced (using America's peculiar legal arithmetic) to imprisonment for life plus ninety-nine years. Their families, each of which contained several millionaires, reneged on most of the lives-saving fees they had promised Darrow. In 1936 Loeb was killed by a fellow convict who claimed that he had acted in self-defense, Loeb having sought to have sexual relations with him—a statement instantly accepted by the *Chicago Daily*

Nathan Leopold and Richard Loeb (at center), awaiting trial in 1924. From Maureen McKernan, *The Crime and Trial of Leopold and Loeb* (London: Allen and Unwin, 1925).

News, which reported that "Richard Loeb, a brilliant college student and master of the English language, today ended a sentence with a proposition." Leopold was released in 1958; he went to Puerto Rico, where he did charitable work and, after three years, got married and died from natural causes in 1971.

Hurshell kept the engine running while I was looking around. I couldn't have chosen a better cabbie. I say that, not only because he is so genial and so careful of me, but also because he has heard and read a lot about Al Capone. I didn't need to explain that the next two addresses on the scrap of paper I gave him were associated with Capone—and he tells me of two others, saying that we can "include them in the tour" ("—no extra," he adds, referring to the fact that I have agreed a roundtrip payment with him, the fare meter off).

As we drive to the first of the now-four places, he chuckles and says: "From what I've been told—it may not be gospel-truth, mind—Mr. Capone wouldn't have made the grade in my occupation, where you need some learning of geography. I've heard tell that one time he asked what street Canada was on—and the guy he asked, understandably nervous about belittling Mr. Capone, told him the name of a street. And another time he admitted he didn't know what state Vermont was in." Hurshell's unrestrained enjoyment of the anecdotes adds to my enjoyment of them.

On South Wabash Avenue he slows down, apparently deaf to the hysterical hootings from the vehicles behind, and, pointing to a demolition site, murmurs, "One legal wrecking among hundreds in this city. Wouldn't surprise me if Chicago is the biggest employer of those guys that swing them big old iron balls." He says that what we are looking at used to be number 2222.

In 1919, a month or so before the start of Prohibition, Johnny Torrio, a Sicilian-born gangster who was pleased to be called "The Brain," acquired and furbished the building as a pleasure dome of booze, gambling, and prostitution. The street number, changed into poker players' slang, gave the place its name: The Four Deuces.

A few years earlier Torrio had accepted an invitation from his uncle by marriage, "Big Jim" Colosimo, to move from New York to Chicago and help with the Colosimo wholesale prostitution business. Soon establishing himself as Big Jim's deputy, he had meanwhile begun setting

Johnny Torrio: a 1925 newspaper photo. The picture was taken following an ambush, which explains the loose bandage around his neck.

up businesses of his own. In the spring of 1920 Torrio took two actions
among several: one, which he presumably thought hard if not long
about, was to engage a New York hit man to pay a flying visit to Chicago and murder Big Jim; the other, which, taken on the spur of the
moment, had extraordinary consequences, was to invite a psychopathic
crony to move from New York to Chicago and help with the Torrio
(largely ex-Colosimo) conglomerate of criminal businesses. The crony,
who was of Neapolitan parentage, fat faced and barrel chested, had
only recently celebrated his coming of age, which in those days was
twenty-one. His name was Al Capone.

Starting menially—as a tout for trade outside the Four Deuces, a
bartender and prostitutes' bodyguard within the premises, and a

Al Capone, ca. 1925.

bouncer of awkward customers from them—Capone rose through the ranks and by 1925 was Torrio's deputy. In the spring of that year, Torrio, having miraculously escaped injury from an ambush by trigger happy and revengeful gangsters and having also miraculously recovered from half a dozen bullet wounds sustained during a subsequent ambush, decided that, since his enemies were likely to be third-time lucky, it was prudent to retire somewhere, anywhere, a long way from Chicago.

Consequently, Capone, still just young enough to be described as an infant criminal prodigy, became the Mr. Big of the city's underworld. And in a very short time he became Mr. Far Bigger. And before long he was Mr. Biggest, nonpareil throughout the then forty-eight states of the Union—which, as American criminals had the inestimable blessing of Prohibition, one of the stupidly unforeseen effects of which was to ally thirsty, otherwise-lawful citizens with thirst-quenching thugs, meant the world.

Andrew Volstead, prime mover of the Eighteenth Amendment, the prohibitive one, was in his unthinking way more mischievous then Genghis Khan and Attila the Hun put together. Top American criminals, so many of whom take Sundays off to worship a God, confess to petty sins, and enjoy good clean fun in the bosom of their families, should pester the Pope to declare Volstead their patron saint—Saint Andrew of the Yellow Medicine County Tea Rooms, perhaps. Just one meddlesome politician among a surfeit of politicians of outstanding inability—though no worse than the majority of British MPs, an ever-increasing majority as politics becomes a straight-from-school profession instead of a progression from some other kind of work well done.

Hurshell's other extra stop is on the road named after Anton Cermak, the crooked mayor of Chicago until 1933, when, while motoring in Miami, he was fatally shot by a Sicilian, Giuseppe Zangara, who may have intended to kill the man sitting next to him in the open touring car, President-elect Franklin Delano Roosevelt. One side of this stretch of Cermak Road could be used for location scenes, caftan-covered passersby and all, of a movie situated in downtown Beirut. "They sure have swung those big old iron balls hereabouts," Hurshell says. He waves his hand at an empty space adjoining a Burger King and tells me that the Metropole Hotel once stood there.

When Al Capone took over from Johnny Torrio, he rented one of that hotel's floors as his headquarters. In 1927 he moved across the street to the Lexington Hotel. Although he only rented its fourth floor, he behaved as though the whole building belonged to him: his sentries, made lopsided by their underarm artillery, patrolled the lobby, lounged at the secondary entrances, and sat on gilt-spindled chairs beside the elevator doors. One of Capone's biographers, John Kobler, says that Room 430, which Capone called his salon, was "the nerve-centre of his multifarious activities"—"Cash was stacked around Room 430 in padlocked canvas bags, awaiting its transfer to a bank under fictitious names. . . . In the oval vestibule a crest enclosing the initials A.C. had been inlaid in the oak parquet. At the left a bathroom contained an immense sunken tub with gold-plated faucets and ceramic tiles of Nile green and royal purple. An ancient Oriental rug covered the floor of the salon, and the high ceiling was embossed with an elaborate foliage design. A chandelier of amber and smoked glass shed a soft light."

I wonder how Room 430 is decorated now. Less opulently, I guess, basing the guess only partly on the lackluster outward appearance of the cube-shaped building, which lacks glass in most of its windows on one side—also, presumably, in the larger ground-floor windows that are covered with graffiti-daubed plywood. Some time after 1931, when Capone terminated his tenancy, having been sentenced to eleven years' imprisonment for income-tax evasion, the Lexington became a brothel, large even by Chicago standards, and then a flophouse for itinerants till 1980 when it was closed by court order. The last I heard, it had been bought by an organization that trained women for construction work, and the intention was to turn it into apartments, shops, and "a women's museum."

Perhaps that intention is being fulfilled by the half-dozen work-men, no women, who, presumably taking a break from their labors, are sitting on the step at the main entrance, chewing unwieldy buns from the Burger King. I enquire of the man at one end of the sedentary line, and he, having inefficiently swallowed his mouthful of bun, says: "I just paint what I'm paid to paint. I don't ask why I'm painting what I'm told to paint." He takes another intemperate bite from his bun, signifying that he has nothing to add, and as his colleagues are still engrossed in their respective buns, I walk back to the cab.

Hurshell jogs my memory of a Lexington "news" story that was covered by both BBC and Independent television news programs. In the late 1980s an American television personality named Geraldo Riviera had the idea—bright if he was thinking only of publicity, stupid if not—that something called "Capone's Treasure" was hidden behind a wall in the Lexington's basement. To accept the idea, first it was necessary to believe that Capone had taken the trouble to store rainy-day things in the basement and found a wonderfully trustworthy bricklayer to turn an open space into a secret vault and, then, that neither while he was in prison nor afterward, neither he nor any of his surviving henchmen had thought to remove the treasure. Never minding such quibbles, Mr. or Senor Riviera devoted most of a program to the destruction of a per-fectly good wall, and when the space behind proved to be empty, showed that he didn't know the difference between nothing and something by saying, "As it turns out, we haven't found very much," and made the worst of a bad job by breaking into song—"Chicago, Chicago," of course.

On the way to the first of the Capone-associated sites on my list, Hurshell sums up bootleggers: "They were nasty, sure—but I guess they, their customers too, considered that they were doing business like any other business, like selling chocolate bars nobody was supposed to buy."

We stop, though it is illegal, near the intersection of Michigan Avenue and Randolph Street. I don't know if this is the officially recognized center of Chicago, but it feels as if it is, just as Grand Army Plaza feels like the center of Manhattan and, though Charing Cross is the place in London from which milestones are measured, Piccadilly Circus feels like the center of my own city. Grant Park is on the right, Lake Michigan beyond; facing us, to the north, is the phalanx of skyscrapers (some of them, though none of the tallest, as handsome as any I have ever seen); and farther up the avenue, which is also called the Magnificent Mile from where the skyscrapers start, is the Knickerbocker. Across the avenue, to our left, is the massive Public Library. On this Grant Park side is the entrance to the subway leading to the suburban railway.

At lunchtime on Monday, June 9, 1930—a very hot day, though not as sweltering as this one—Alfred "Jake" Lingle, a thirty-eight-year-old, sixty-five-dollar-a-week police reporter for the *Chicago Tribune,* bought the *Daily Racing Form* from the newsstand in front of the Public Library, lit a cigar, and walked across to the subway. He trotted down the steps and walked toward the east ramp. He was one of hundreds of people, most of them men, intending to catch the 1:30 train to the Washington Park racetrack. He may have been aware of a slight commotion behind him, caused by a nattily dressed young man who was elbowing his way through the crowd. The dapper but rude young man, having come abreast of Lingle, produced a revolver and fired it, point blank, through Lingle's head, killing him instantly, then dropped the gun and dashed out of the subway. Fourteen persons either witnessed his killing of Lingle or had their attention drawn to him by the hurriedness of his retreat; all said they would recognize him if they ever saw him again. Next day the *Tribune* trumpeted:

The meaning of this murder is plain. It was committed in reprisal and in an attempt to intimidate. Mr. Lingle was a police reporter and an exceptionally well informed one. His personal friendships included the highest police officials, and the contacts of his work made him familiar to most of the big and little fellows of gangland. What made him valuable to his newspaper marked him as dangerous to the killers. . . . The Tribune accepts this challenge. It is war. There will be casualties, but that is to be expected, it being war.

The *Tribune* was the first casualty arising from Lingle's death. Even before announcements that rewards for information about the murderer offered by all of the Chicago papers and by some civic groups totaled $55,000, information about the victim began altering the perception of him as Jake the Martyr to Lingle the Fixer, the Blackmailer, the Double-Dealer. He had wined and dined and "lent" money to high-ranking policemen, had been particularly hospitable and generous to the highest ranking, Commissioner Russell and Deputy Commissioner Stege. His boastfulness about his constabularian intimacies—about favors he had arranged, and could arrange, under the Old (Police) Pals Act—had led many criminals to believe that he was "Chicago's unofficial chief of police," and that reputation had helped him achieve success in the brothel-protection racket. There was evidence that he had acted as intermediary between gang leaders, including Capone, and local politicians, also that he had retailed the business secrets of certain gangs to their closest rivals.

It is hard to believe that not a solitary soul at the *Tribune* was aware of Lingle's extra-journalistic activities till he was no longer on the payroll. Apparently one or two of the paper's investigative reporters had asked him, more from envy than with suspicion, how he was able to afford a palatial house in the suburbs (that he rarely visited, preferring to spend weeknights in a permanently rented room in a downtown hotel), a summer bungalow in Indiana, a straight-from-the-showroom motorcar and a chauffeur to drive it, holidays in places other than Indiana, and thousand-dollar wagers at racetracks—and they had swallowed whatever explanation he had given, either that he had inherited a fortune from his father (who, it turned out, had left him five hundred dollars) or that he had made a killing on the stock market (actually, he and his dear old chum, Police Commissioner Russell, with whom he shared a brokerage account, had lost a fortune in share dealings).

The *Tribune* had to cancel the declaration of war against gangland, being too heavily engaged in a war of the internecine kind, trying to defend itself, and retaliating, against the barrage of Lingle-of-the-*Tribune* stories in the other Chicago papers. Its most spectacular counterattack was a series of articles that told tales about the shady moonlighting ventures of a half-dozen non-*Tribune* newspapermen.

The writer of the articles, who seems to have been as reckless with regard to the continuance of his life as he was incautious of libel, subsequently turned up, unannounced and unprotected, at Al Capone's summer house on an island off the coast of Florida and, telling the bodyguards that he knew that the owner was in residence, insisted on seeing him. Capone, nice as pie (or, as he preferred, pizza), jovially answered questions, many of which carried the implication that he had arranged the murder of Jake Lingle. When asked if he knew who had committed the crime, he said, "Why ask me?"—then added, "The Chicago police know who killed Jake." He insisted that Jake had been his friend "up to the very day he died," that he had "absolutely not" had a row with him, and that the story (said to have emanated from an indiscreet, presently still-breathing member of his gang) that he and Lingle had fallen out over the latter's welshing on a deal was "Bunk—*bunk.*" He claimed that he paid retainers to "plenty" of reporters and near the end of the interview said: "Let me give you a hot tip— lay off Chicago and the money-hungry reporters. You're right, and because you're right, you're wrong. . . . No one will ever realize just how big it is, so lay off." Following the publication of the interview, not only in the *Tribune,* Capone said that it was a fabrication.

Soon afterward, a grand jury examined the allegations made against the six non-*Tribune* newspapermen in the *Tribune* series and declared— rather strangely, considering that several of the allegations had since been confirmed—that there was no support for any of the allegations. Also rather strangely, not one of the men named in the series sued for libel.

In the spring of 1931 a young criminal named Leo Brothers, who had been hiding out in Chicago since leaving his hometown of St. Louis (where he was wanted for arson, bombing, murder, and robbery), stood trial for and was found guilty of the murder of Jake Lingle. The *Tribune* was the only Chicago paper that agreed with the verdict; others insinuated that Brothers was either the innocent victim of a frame-up or a man who, with little to lose, had volunteered to be a patsy on the understanding that he would not be executed and that he would receive a golden handshake as soon as he was released from prison. The doubters considered that their doubts were supported by the jury's rider to their verdict, which, unarguably peculiar, was that the man they had decided was a cold-blooded murderer was to be let off lightly, with a prison sentence that, if he behaved himself, would last eight years. Brothers, looking happy but not surprised, bragged, "I can do that standing on my head." The prosecution case had depended on eyewitness evidence: seven of the fourteen persons who had described a man to the police immediately after the murder said that they were sure Brothers was that man, but none of the certain seven was among those who had seen the murder being done.

A few weeks after the trial, part of a body was found in a burnt-out house a dozen miles from Chicago; it was identified as having been a salient constituent of "Mike de Pike" Heitler, a Capone whoremaster who had recently been given the sack. A letter he had entrusted to his daughter, telling her that it was to be opened only in the event of his death from unnatural causes, named eight members of the Capone gang as conspirators in the murder of Lingle and described a meeting held shortly before the murder at which Capone had criticized Lingle as being a double-crosser and assured everyone present, Mike de Pike among them, "Jake is going to get his."

Whether or not Lingle got his fatal comeuppance at the behest of Capone is still, and I expect will remain, a moot point. The question strikes me as being of only academic interest. If whoever gave the order had not given it at that time or shortly afterward, some other aggrieved party would surely have given it because Lingle had pushed his luck far too far and in far too many criminous directions. He was a thoroughly deserving victim. Hurshell agrees with me. "From all I've heard about that Mr. Lingle," he says, "the gentleman took a really alarming number of risks to his health."

Having driven to the top of the Magnificent Mile, we turn left and, after Hurshell has worked hard at the steering wheel to squiggle around a rash of road works, arrive on the low-2000s stretch of North Clark Street. "Moran's Territory, huh?" he says, still panting from his exertions.

"Not Mr. Moran?"

"Well, no, sir, " he says, having considered. "I mean, referring to someone called Bugs as Mr. don't sound right, wouldn't you agree? No disrespect, mind."

He parks across the street from a blank space bounded at the back by a neat private hedge, where number 2122 used to stand. I knew that the building had been pulled down; Hurshell tries to work out when but can get no closer than "say late in the '60s, give or take." I am surprised that the neighborhood is quite nice. The several-storied Victorian houses directly south of the space have porches with Doric columns; those houses and farther, slightly less imposing ones, remind me of the architecture in squares near the museums in South Kensington. From reading about what happened at number 2122 on St. Valentine's Day 1929, I had gathered that the surroundings were squalid; perhaps I misread between the lines of the accounts, taking it for granted that the area around the happenings was scenically appropriate to them. Most narrative writing has gaps that readers have to fill in from their imaginations, and we are not always imaginative enough.

George (better known as "Bugs" on account of his dangerous eccentricities) Moran had become leader of the North Side Gang by virtue of the fact that three of the previous successive leaders had died young— the first two (Dion O'Banion and Hymie Weiss) from bullets fired on behalf of rival gang leaders (Johnny Torrio and Al Capone) and the third (Vincent "Schemer" Drucci) from bullets fired at close range by a detective who had arrested him and become peeved with his chutzpah.

Although Capone had reason to be grateful to Moran, who was among the ambushers who had very nearly killed Torrio, causing him to retire, he had at least three general reasons for determining that Bugs should "get his": *revenge* (for instance, because in 1926 Moran had led a convoy of cars past the Hawthorne Inn, Capone's headquarters in the suburb of Cicero, he and the following riders splintering the façade of the premises to matchwood with machine-gun fire and giving Capone, lying on the floor, a splitting headache); *pique* (for instance, because Moran, who didn't hold with prostitution, had publicly turned down Capone's request to open brothels on the North Side, telling reporters: "Anyone who deals in flesh is lower than a snake's belly. Can't Capone get that through his thick skull?"); and *avarice* (the most important reason, because with the extermination of Bugs the North Side Gang would have run out of leaders, and Capone could take over the one remaining bit of Chicago that he coveted).

One must speak of the Capone plan rather than Capone's plan because it was so ingenious and yet so simple, a slaughtering equivalent of the invention of the wheel, that it must have come as an inspiration to someone wise enough to realize that embellishment would only blemish it. A gangster of Detroit—who, so far as Moran knew, had no links with Capone—offered him a shipment of liquor at such a reasonable price that a deal was struck on the spot. Arrangements were made: delivery at 10:30 on the morning of February 14, St. Valentine's Day, which that year, 1929, fell on a Thursday. (Sadly, no one knows if it was the planner who chose the festive, sly-messages-to-sweethearts day, chuckling with admiration at his delightful sense of whimsy.) The delivery address was 2122 North Clark Street.

That was one of the North Siders' warehouses. It was a single-story, redbrick building, sixty feet wide and twice as long, that had been intended as a garage; the floor was of concrete, the whitewash on the walls had turned yellow. Tall, wide doors at the back opened on to a loading area. The glass panel in the front door had been painted black, as had the top of the large window to the right of the door. A black-on-white sign filled the bottom of the window:

S-M-C Cartage CO
Shipping   Packing
Phone Diversey 1471
Long Distance Hauling

On St. Valentine's morning there were four empty trucks inside, one jacked up and being repaired by one of the six gangsters, who, unlike three of their fellows, had arrived on time. Also there, just for the thrill of being in the company of real gangsters, was an optician who cannot have been as stupid as his presence suggests, for he had a paper qualification that entitled him to call himself a doctor. The car-mechanical gangster's German shepherd dog, called Highball, was tethered to the incapacitated truck.

A black Cadillac pulled up at the front of the warehouse. Many of the Chicago Police Department's unmarked cars were of the same make and color. Five men got out of the car; two of them wore police uniform. They all rushed through the door, which seems to have been left on the latch. They lined the six North Siders and the groupie optician against a wall, facing it. Two of the intruders produced submachine guns from under their overcoats (it was a bitterly cold day) and, using the weapons as if they were garden hoses, sprayed the occupants with bullets, lavishly killing all of them. Highball howled.

The dog was still howling when two men came out of the building. They had their hands up because the two men behind them, those dressed as policemen, were prodding their ribs with pistols. The third civilian, apparently a detective, followed. The five men got into the black Cadillac and drove away, south for a block, then to the west.

The withdrawal was watched by, among others, Bugs Moran and two other fortunately unpunctual North Siders.

Within hours of what had been immutably christened the St. Valentine's Day Massacre, Moran mournfully insisted, "Only Capone kills like that"—Capone, who just happened to be out of town, cheekily insisted, "The only man who kills like that is Bugs"—and the local Prohibition administrator, a fool named Silloway, blithely insisted, though he hadn't a tittle of evidence in support of the insistence, that the killers were not pretend policemen but real ones. Soon afterward, someone having explained the difference between an uninspired hunch and an undeniable fact to Silloway, he lied that he had been misquoted; as he was a civil servant, he was not given the sack but was transferred to a relatively lawful district. Eventually it was established that the massacre had been ordered by Capone, and three members of his posse were identified beyond a doubt. But no one was ever tried for the crime.

On the eve of the seventh anniversary of the event, Jack "Machine Gun" McGurn, who was one of the killers, perhaps the commander of the operation, was himself injected with far more bullets than were needed to kill him—probably by gunmen acting on the orders of Bugs Moran. He would have needed to employ outside help. Although he, the prime target of the Capone plan, had been physically unscathed by its execution, the plan had achieved all three of the known reasons why Capone had set it in motion. Moran's middle management had been sorely depleted, his prestige had crumbled, and, for that reason and because an inference from the massacre was that opponents of Capone were so in need of life assurance that no assurance company would be interested in their custom, many of the North Siders had either evacuated the district or decided that, since Capone certainly couldn't be licked, they had better join him.

It is good to know that things went from bad to worse for Bugs and that some of the worst things were long lasting. From 1946 he served ten years' imprisonment for robbing a bank messenger of an amount of money that, in the good old days, he would have treated as loose change. As soon as he was released he was rearrested for another robbery but served only one of the ten years he was sentenced to, because an illness from which he had begun to suffer during his first imprisonment proved fatal.

While I was wandering around where the S-M-C Cartage Company used to be, Hurshell remembered something, and as soon as I get back to the cab he tells me what it is: that when the building was torn down, an entrepreneur had the bricks of the firing squad wall transported "across the lake to some place in Canada" and relaid as a false wall in the gents' lavatory of a Roaring Twenties nightclub he owned: "I guess because lady customers felt left out, they were let into the toilet on certain nights a week (don't ask me how that arrangement worked, sir), but I read somewhere that the attraction didn't prove attractive, and the Canadian gentleman had the wall pulled down again, and he offered single bricks for sale at a thousand bucks each—*each*, would you believe? I'd be surprised if he sold a great many of them bricks."

Our next stop, the last, isn't far—north along Clark and onto Lincoln Avenue, which branches off to the right. Number 2433. Again I am surprised by the niceness of a neighborhood. Perhaps "nice" is not the word: neighborliness?—yes, that's better. Too many fast-food places, of course, each of a different Latin or oriental nationality, but lots of small needed shops too; most of the people out walking look as if they have walked no more than a block or two, only to shop or just to stroll; some of them say hi to me, as if hoping that I will ask them the way somewhere. I wonder if the pub-cum-café across the street from number 2433 is called the Jury Room because it *is* across the street—from the Biograph.

Seeing the cinema gives me a very odd feeling. It is like looking at a complete stranger I know well. I have seen so many snaps taken of the Biograph in the summer of 1934 that the building has become one-dimensional and glossy in my mind's eye. But here it *is*—not only here but also hardly altered since it gained a kind of stardom. The scroll-topped marquee, serrated with little light bulbs, appears to be the same one; "Essaness," the name of the company that ran the place then, has gone from above "BIOGRAPH," and there is no canvas valance.

The valance that hung from the marquee in the summer of 1934 proclaimed "COOLED BY REFRIGERATION" in letters larger than those on the placards advertising the main feature, which, on Sunday, July 22, was *Manhattan Melodrama,* starring Clark Gable as a murderer and

William Powell as his best friend, the district attorney required to pros-
ecute him. The duty-versus-friendship movie was a big hit, but as that
Sunday night was broiling hot, the cinema would not have been packed
but for the valanced enticement.

Sitting in a back row, flanked by two women, was a dark-haired, slack-
mouthed young man named John Dillinger. (While I was in New York,
I had lunch with Michael Brown—who, using just two of his many
talents, has composed some splendid songs, including the one about
Lizzie Borden, "You Can't Chop Your Poppa Up in Massachusetts"—
and he assured me that before Dillinger became famous as a bank rob-
ber and escaper from jails, his name was pronounced "*Dillin*-Ger" and
that wireless newscasters altered the pronunciation to "*Dillin*-Jer," chiming with the name of a pistol, Derringer, and therefore appropriate to
his exploits.)

One of Dillinger's Biographical companions was a Romanian-born
woman presently calling herself Anna Sage. He didn't know it, of course,
but she had betrayed him to Melvin Purvis, the agent in charge of the
Chicago office of the FBI, on the understanding that if the betrayal
caused the capture of Dillinger, who had recently risen to the top of
the FBI's league-table of public enemies, she would receive a reward of
ten thousand dollars, along with Purvis's invaluable help in fighting a
deportation order against her, she having been found guilty, not for
the first time, of running a disorderly house. The other woman with
Dillinger was Polly Hamilton, a prostitute Sage had "arranged" for him.

The movie was not quite over when Dillinger, guessing (correctly)
that there would be no commutation of the death sentence on Clark
Gable and wanting to avoid the after-performance crush, indicated to
his companions that it was time to go. They filed out into the foyer.

Mrs. Sage was wearing a skirt that, under street lighting, looked more
red than its real color, orange, hence the title, the "Woman in Red,"
that was soon attached to her. It was as well that Melvin Purvis, less
than perfect in some respects, downright useless in others, was gifted
with an excellent eye for color, as Mrs. Sage was wearing the skirt as a
"marker"—so that Purvis, stationed across the street, holding a cigar
in one hand and matches in the other, would know who she was and
that the man next to her was Dillinger. Come to think of it, which

Purvis hadn't, it was also as well that no trio composed of a man and two women, one wearing an orange or red skirt, emerged from the Biograph before the Dillinger trio did or that the Dillinger trio did not stay till the end of the movie and then joined the after-performance crush, else Purvis's plan would have turned into a fiasco, and perhaps more innocent persons than the two actually wounded by ricocheting FBI bullets would have been injured.

But it *was* the awaited trio that emerged. Now Purvis was supposed to light his cigar as a signal to the dozens of other FBI men who for the past hour or so had been standing to the left and right of him, pretending to be casual loiterers while staring intently at his cigar and matches. The trouble was that Purvis (one feels like saying Poor Purvis— but no, he does not deserve sympathy) got such a fit of the shakes that he was quite unable to strike a match. Some of the agents, though sure that they had seen Dillinger out of the corner of their staring-at-Purvis eyes, kept on waiting for the signal; others, equally sure that they had caught sight of Dillinger, assumed that they must have missed the signal while blinking and rushed toward him, thinking that there were behind colleagues who had not blinked.

Dillinger started to run—to the right of the cinema—his head down, his back hunched. Meanwhile, Purvis, who had not thought to leave his jacket open, tore the buttons off in his effort to get hold of the guns tucked in his belt, and some of the other agents, quicker on the draw, began firing at Dillinger. He staggered into an alley. More bullets burrowed through him. He fell dead. His blood puddled the ground, but soon after his body had been carried away, the ground was made dry by the hankie dipping of souvenir hunters.

Membership of the already flourishing John Dillinger Fan Club increased dramatically; the notion that he was a latter-day Robin Hood became more generally accepted; people put out of work, made hungry by the Great Depression, thought they understood what had made him a criminal.

I think of Michael Brown's sweet little song, "Where Are You, Johnny?" and remember a few lines of the lyrics:

The streets are full of sobbing people again,
The banks have started robbing people again.

Give us a headline,
One to remember,
Life on the breadline
Is such a bore.

I only go into the foyer of the Biograph. There is no point in going farther as this cinema, like nearly all surviving ones, has become "multiplex"; the auditorium has been divided to make three screens. I hope the successors of Essaness have the sense to show *Manhattan Melodrama* in one of the three each July 22.

There is a plaque, bronze looking, on the right-hand outside wall—THIS PROPERTY HAS BEEN PLACED ON THE NATIONAL REGISTER OF HISTORIC PLACES BY THE UNITED STATES DEPARTMENT OF THE INTERIOR. Not just because it has survived, surely?

The building that makes the nearer side of the alley is said to be Park West FOODS but looks to me like a liquor store; the building that makes the far side is a Mexican restaurant. The alley, which is littered with squashy things that I, wishing to enjoy my dinner, don't want to identify, has no memorial to the man who died here. Perhaps some of the graffiti, which is all in languages I don't know, refers to Dillinger. The day after his death, someone—a local poetic policeman, according to one account—chalked a verse on a wall of the alley:

Stranger, stop and wish me well,
Just say a prayer for my soul in Hell.
I was a good fellow, most people said,
Betrayed by a woman all dressed in red.

When I come out of a good bookshop a few doors down from the Biograph, I notice that Hurshell appears to be doing a paper-tearing act within the confines of the front of his cab. By the time I rejoin him, he has not merely cleared up the mess of many separated sheets of newspapers but has miraculously made the mess disappear. He has set off back to the Knickerbocker before he hands me two neatly torn strips of newsprint, one from the front page of the Metro section of the *Chicago Tribune,* the other the continuation of the story. "Now that's what I call a coincidence, sir," he says—and after looking at the headline, DILLINGER DEATH MASK A STEAL AT $10,000, I agree with him. The story refers to an auction that took place the previous day in Chicago. The reporter, David Silverman, explains:

> Just hours after FBI agents had gunned down Public Enemy No. 1 in front of [sic] the Biograph Theater, viewing the bank robber's body became theater of another sort. In a basement examining room . . . in the Cook County coroner's office . . . hundreds of politicians, police and the public elbowed their way in for a glimpse. During the night the room was cleared. Unidentified workmen then greased Dillinger's face, layered it twice with plaster of Paris and walked away with the only known death-masks made of a twentieth century criminal. . . . Some say it was a rogue band of students from a local embalming school, others say it was a pair of men from a dental supply company who later sent J. Edger Hoover a death-mask of his own. But the stories are merely part of the gangster legend that has grown to make Dillinger the Elvis of crimeland.
>
> Yesterday, the legend grew once again as one of the two masks vanished into the hands of an unidentified British collector of rare and unusual things who snapped it up at auction for a mere $10,000. "Just another American treasure going overseas to a foreign country," said Edward Mueller, a 74-year-old Chicagoan in the packed auction room of Leslie Hindman auctioneers. "I'm surprised that there wasn't a fight with some Japanese buyer, some bigwig who was looking for something to go with his Monets," Mueller said.

I am pleased to tell Hurshell that I haven't the faintest idea who the unidentified British collector is, and only then does he offer his opinion: "Seems to me that anyone prepared to spend ten grand on a death mask ought to be spending his money on brain surgery." We are at the hotel by now, and having settled up, I thank him and say goodbye, shaking his shyly extended hand.

My second part of a day in Chicago began early. I was the first customer in the restaurant. There was no sign of a waiter, let alone of a headwaiter to tell me where I couldn't sit, and I sat at the table farthest from the door, beside a window. Eventually a small, knobbly waiter appeared and eventually spotted me. I ordered coffee and eggs, bacon, and sauté potatoes, with plenty of toast, and asked the waiter to take away four-fifths of the newspaper that I had tripped over, very nearly injuring myself, when I came out of my room.

Before my breakfast arrived, another customer entered. I am not good at guessing ages, but I reckon he was in his mid-sixties. His hair, black peppered with gray, was very nicely cut, but his eyebrows were untidy. He looked to me like an Italian tycoon, but the second part of that impression was largely owed to his gray, tycoon's suit, which was ostentatiously hand stitched. I got a close-up view of the hand stitching because, though he could have sat at any other of the dozens of empty tables, he chose to sit at the one next to me.

I waited, expecting him to catch my eye and say good morning, but it seemed that he was gregarious but impolite. It took him some time to arrange himself—or rather his suit, so that no unintended creases marred the bespokeness. I could tell that his socks, which were of black silk with little red horses on them, like his tie, were held up by suspenders and was wondering if the suspenders matched the socks when he, his attention arrested by something in his newspaper, started chatting tetchily—not to me, as I thought at first, but to himself. Although I heard everything he said, and understood most of it, I shall respect the intended privacy of his one-sided conversation.

The waiter brought me my breakfast, then turned to the tycoon, who was still chatting away. The waiter coughed interruptingly, and the tycoon, looking up with a start, said: "Yeah? You got problems? Bring me the yewzhel."

"Yewzhel, M'sieur? You mean moozli?"

"No, I do not mean moozli, for crying out loud. The yewzhel: spelt U S—as in the United States, this damned country, for God's sake—followed by a U and an E and an L. Yewzhel."

"I am here new," the waiter hoped he explained.

"Oh, sure—new since this same time yesterday morning, huh? Well, I'll say this just the once more. Listening?" He rattled off the components of the yewzhel: "Fresh—and I mean fresh—orange juice, decaf, wholemeal crackers, no-fat spread, Perrier"—and then, punching the left side of his chest not quite hard enough to disarrange the mono-grammed hankie in his breast pocket, moaned: "Holy cow—this is exactly the kind of irritation my doctors say I've got to avoid." Dismissively to the waiter: "Farewell, Miguel."

The waiter, a confused bundle of nerves by now, scampered away, scribbling on his notepad as he went. I shouldn't have been surprised if, once he had reached the sanctuary of the kitchen, he asked the cook for a single portion of yewzhel with a side order of holy cow.

Meanwhile, the tycoon, having caught sight of my plate, stared aghast at it, exclaiming, "What the hell's that you're eating?"

I told him.

"And you're aiming to drop dead from chlorestoril, right? As soon as possible, right?"

I, till a moment ago enjoying the eggs, bacon, and sauté potatoes, said that new research indicated that the cholesterol scare lacked sub-stance.

"And, oh sure, you believe everything you read?"

I pointed out that he had probably read what scared him about cholesterol—and he, not at all disconcerted, replied: "All depends *where* you read things you'd maybe rather not know. I read the *Wall Street Joinal*." He waved his copy as clear proof, not only that he read it, but also that I didn't have long to live. "Never lets me down. Have to admit, though, that it got me riled just now."

"About what?" I asked, though I had a pretty good idea.

"Oh, the yewzhel," he said, flapping the least ringed one of his mani-cured hands frustratedly, and then changed the subject to something equally upsetting: "That frigging un-American waiter . . . You foreign too?"

"English."

"English?"

"From England."

"England . . . Oh, yeah." His expression brightened as he remem-bered things about England: "Coral, right? William Hill. Ladbroke's."

Feeling pleased with myself at having passed the name-association test, I said, "Mecca," the only other English bookmaking firm I know of, and asked him how he came to be so particularly well informed.

We were still completely alone in the big room, but he lowered his voice to explain that he was "part of the racing game," that he had sold a horseracing track he owned in Idaho to "a syndicate—don't misunderstand that word—of Chicago . . . er . . . businessmen" who had retained his services as a consultant.

He may have intended to tell me more, but at that moment a younger man, just as Italian looking and wearing a gray suit with quite as much hand stitching, came into the restaurant, and the first tycoon shouted at him: "Hey, Alfredo, so what kept you? Traffic jams at 7:30 A.M. already? Forgive my mirth." (He hadn't smiled; still wasn't smiling.) "If the service here wasn't so frigging slow, I'd have finished eating and been on my way to the airport."

He gestured in my direction—rather condescendingly, I thought—and said: "This guy here, he's from England, would you believe?"

Alfredo muttered, "Mecca," and the first tycoon said, "Yeah, just like he just remanded me. But take a look at what he's eating, will you?"

Alfredo, who had sat next to him by now, took a look. Actually, there was little to see; I was mopping the plate with a slice of buttered toast. But still, Alfredo tutted and muttered: "Criminal. Like as if suicide, which in my opinion should be classed like murder in the first degree. Ought to be a law."

I don't think he had looked at me, only at my plate, and now he turned away from it with a shudder and whispered urgently to the first tycoon what sounded like "five six eight nine one." That, or some fraction of the esoteric remark, surprised or worried the first tycoon, who asked, "Five six—you sure you got that right?" and instantly added an imperative though redundant "Schtum" to warn Alfredo of my nearness.

The rest of the conversation was meant to be inaudible to me. I caught an occasional digit, but as, say, six is, generally speaking, of no more significance to me than, say, eight, I soon concentrated on my toast and what Americans think of as marmalade. It is like sweet gravy. The two tycoons were still conversing numerically as I got up to leave.

The first of them had the good grace to break off in the middle of what sounded as if it was going to become "seven" to say, "Yeah, and you have a nice day too, English," though I had certainly not expressed the hope that *he* would have a nice one, and then, without pause except to take in a deep breath, screamed a question at the nearest chandelier, making it quiver: "Where in hell's name is that son-of-a-bitch of a waiter guy?"

The last-retired chief editor of the Oxford English Dictionaries has been quoted as saying that English English and American English are diverging at such a rate that before long they will be entirely different languages. If he did say that, he spoke nonsense; the two brands of English are *con*verging: I am sure that there are now fewer differences between them than there are, for instance, between the English of the remaining English citizens of London and that of inhabitants of rural Northumberland. Perhaps he spoke not of divergence but of mutual extinction, which, frighteningly, seems possible. Most residents of some once-very-English cities know only a few words of English, and many of the remainder treat English as a second language—and the front page of this morning's paper carries the paradoxical news that ethnic minorities outnumber the majority in more than fifty American cities. Presently, though, the only real difference between the two brands of English is that each has a few extra-to-the-other words, and most of those words are so rarely used that anyone supposed to have them on the tip of his native tongue would probably need to look them up in his native dictionary.

I think it is true to say that all of *my* incomprehensions have arisen from the pronunciation of names. On the Sunday afternoon while I was in Cleveland, everyone else seemed anxious to know the latest score in a football game between the local team and that of Cincinnati, and I gathered that one team or the other was called the Bangles. When I asked why they were called the Bangles, I was for a while perplexed by the answer, which was that the players wear tiger-striped gear; after considerable mental effort, trying to work out the connection between a carnivorous mammal and an ornamental bracelet, I realized that what I had heard as "*Bang*-les" was what the English would pronounce as "Ben-*gauls*" (not that the English use that plural; we add Bengal to tigers and Lancers, and that's about it).

Mainly because of confusion over a name, I lost almost an hour this morning. After having my breakfast time blighted by the tycoons (and further curtailed by their closeness, for I feared the consequence of lighting an after-breakfast cigarette at point-blank range of such health-conscious associates of *a* syndicate), I thought I might as well take a bus to the Chicago Historical Society, several departments of which I had arranged to visit. I found a bus stop, and it seemed to me that the woman whose assistance I requested told me to "take de bus to de Von." Several buses later, a bus driver nodded when I asked if she was going to the Von; when I asked her to give me a shout when we got there, she said there would be no need as it was the end of the line.

I enjoyed the journey (for much of it, Lake Shore Drive, which, like many other one-sided streets, is beautiful, was on the right; I saw a secondhand bookshop with a sign saying "RARE, MEDIUM and WELL DONE"); but after three-quarters of an hour of it, I, knowing that the historical society was on the Near North Side, not far from Lincoln Avenue, wondered whether it was possible for an area described as being Near the center of Chicago to stretch so Far. This time I asked the driver if she was going to the historical society—and she, giggling so excessively that her eyes watered and the mascara ran, said she hoped not since she was supposed to have had been there quite a while ago. It turned out that the assisting woman at the bus stop should have said, or must have said, "take the bus *going* to"—and that what I had heard as "de Von" is the locals' way of saying "Devon." Presumably that far-northern area of the city got its name from the English county, pronounced *"De-v'n,"* but either from the start or more lately has sounded like—well, what *I* thought it was: a memorial to some Prussian general, so imposing as to have become a landmark on the Near North Side.

The cabbie who drove me back to within a stroll of where I had started from was a miserable sod. He didn't like being a cabbie; he hadn't liked any job he had ever done and couldn't imagine that he would like any job he would ever do; he had emigrated from Greece to America, which he hated, but had no intention of returning to Greece because he hated that country even more than he hated America. He had a large stock of Wise Sayings, one being "When idealism and politics come together, the result is a bloody uprising." It occurred to me that when tomato juice and vodka come together, the result is a bloody Mary, but I didn't have the courage to say so.

Owing to the overlong bus ride, I wasn't able to spend long enough at the historical society, which puts a large modern building to very good use. It is admirable that there are so many, and so many excellent, historical societies in America; disgraceful that there are so few, and no decent ones, in England. Americans are lucky, of course: their history is compact—whereas ours extends too far back, into ages that have little interest because few of the characters can be recognized as *people;* as Groucho Marx very nearly said, if there had been no Venerable Bede, there would still be more than enough of him.

At the back of the Knickerbocker is the John Hancock Center, which, as well as being extraordinarily tall (people *pay* to use the lift to the ninety-fourth floor, some distance from the top), has a basement in which there are shops and a restaurant where, as I eventually discovered, one serves oneself from bowls of salad stuff and is charged for whatever one has taken weighs.

And, through doors from the basement, there is a sunken garden. For me, at any rate, it was made prettier by thousands of inoffensive midges—so white that I couldn't see them when they were zigzagging between me and the very white blouse of a dark-haired girl sitting under a glossy-leafed tree and eating a sandwich, and so very tiny, poor beasties, that they drowned and dissolved when they bumped into people's eyes.

Around one o'clock the bells of the church overlooking the garden chimed songs, not hymns. I suppose the bells are worked mechanically, but the mellow sound reminded me of home (where, on Sundays when the wind is from the southwest, I hear the bells of the parish church). I went into the church, the Fourth Presbyterian of Chicago, and the chiming reminder of home was abetted by the place itself, which is splendidly unsubtle; the stained-glass windows, blitzes of wonderful colors, gave a kind of bonus to my pleasure from looking at the lovely, simple walls.

One of the books I bought at the shop near the Biograph is the *Report of the City Council Committee on Crime of the City of Chicago.* A few extracts from the first couple of pages:

> The treatment of crime in Chicago is wholly inadequate in that many professional criminals escape the penalties of the law and prey at will

upon society; poor and petty criminals are often punished more heavily than is just; practical methods of preventing crime are not applied as extensively as experience warrants and demands.

Professional criminals have built up a system which may be called a "crime trust," with roots running through the police force, the bar, the bondsmen, the prosecutor's office, and political officials.

Professional criminals are recruited from the ranks of delinquent boys, but no adequate means of treatment for such boys is available.

The crime problem is not merely a question of police and courts: it leads to the broader problems of education, home care, a living wage, and industrial democracy.

The report was published in 1915.

To Denver

A s the train pulled out of Union Station (exactly on time: 2:55 P.M.), I was wondering when I could return to Chicago and spend far longer there—in the center and on the North Side, that is; the South Side was not to my liking. So many labels have been stuck on Chicago—"Toddling Town," "Windy City" (I didn't notice the slightest breeze), "Gem of the Prairie," "Queen City of the West," the many made up by the local poet of sorts, Carl Sandburg—that the whole place is hidden from those who haven't been there. Only partly because I didn't know what to expect, much of what I found delighted me.

This route is called the California Zephyr. It runs all the way—nearly two and a half thousand miles—to Oakland, where one gets off and boards a bus into San Francisco, which doesn't seem to have a railway station. I am doing the trip in two stages: all being well, I shall get off at Denver, about a thousand miles from Chicago, at ten minutes to eight tomorrow morning, and catch the next day's train, which is scheduled to leave Denver at nine o'clock that morning; in other words, I shall have a full day in Denver, which, quite beside the point of my decision to spend a day there, is the capital of what I think is the prettiest named of the states, Colorado.

The trains on this route are double-deckers. The ordinary carriages are upstairs, and so is an observation car, with large windows and armchairs facing them, and the restaurant; the café, washrooms, and sleepers are on the bottom deck.

At half past six we crossed the Mississippi, and so I knew we had left Illinois and were in Iowa, "the land beyond." The places we had passed through since leaving Chicago had seemed far less impressive than the great distances between them. I went upstairs and sat in the only vacant chair in the observation car. The elderly man on my right, who was wearing a Stetson and toying with a yo-yo, assured me: "Don't expect any spectacular sights till we reach Denver, and that ain't so spectacular. All you're going to see is corn, soy beans, and cattle shit, not necessarily in that order of picturesqueness." On my left were two teenaged, pregnant, talkative black girls. Neither wore a wedding ring, but one mentioned that she already had two children, and the other topped that by claiming three, and they chatted so esoterically about a medical machine called an ultrascan that all I was able to gather about it, I am glad to say, is that it reveals certain information about a fetus that used to be secret till the delivery.

What with cattle shit, among nicer things, on one side in the observation car and fetuses, among conceptual things, on the other, I am quite surprised when I get to the restaurant that I think that if I am left to my own devices, I can eat a bit of dinner and retain it. Although I am early, the fair-haired man in a yellow anorak sitting across the aisle was earlier: much earlier—he is settling his bill. I order—soon self-consciously because he has tilted across to listen. He sidles from his seat to the one opposite me. It is at times like this in America when I wish I had learned to speak with an American accent. "Mind if I visit?" he says. Lying, I say, "No, of course not."

While I am drinking my soup, not tasting a spoonful of it, he tells me, positive that I am fascinated, that his Christian name is Gregg and that he is "maternally English by birth": his English mother came to America as a "GI bride" soon after the war but has divorced his father "for the usual reason" and returned to England, to York—"a great place:

the Minster cathedral, the Shambles, the candy factory, and you can hardly move for history: take that highwayman guy, Dick Turpin, and his ride to York on his trusty old steed Black Bess—right?" I suggest that, so far as myths are concerned, Dick Turpin is to England what John Dillinger is to America, but he disputes that, saying that "Dillinger was not a class act."

Explaining his firsthand knowledge of York, he says that he has spent several separate months there. The more he talks, the more English he tries to be. He calls his mother "a right good old Yorkshire lass," and when I say something he agrees with, he drawls, "That's pretty damned close to being accurate, old boy." He talks nostalgically of English pubs, of English bitter ale, but when I say that, in comparison with English draught beers, American canned beers aren't beer at all, he says: "Now, now, now—that really is going rather too far: overstepping the jolly old mark, wouldn't you say?" Although he had finished eating before I began, it is I who leave the restaurant first. "Ta-tah," he says.

My reason for having an early dinner was that I had decided to have an early night. I had thought, thinking ahead, that it would be prudent to get some extra hours of sleep. Now, though—I suppose because my brain is exhausted by the effort of holding a conversation with an American latterly talking like a Wodehouse novel—I know that if I don't get to bed quickly, I shall fall untidily asleep on the settee in the roomette and will wake up with, or be woken by, cricks that will make me unfairly grumpy with Denver.

The attendant, only half Sidney's size, brought me early morning coffee. Before he had served everyone, he was serving earlier morning coffee, as we had crossed the border between Nebraska and Colorado, which is the eastern edge of the Mountain Time Zone, an hour behind the Central Zone.

We must have been three or four miles from Denver when I first saw its skyline. The tallness makes the sight surprising, but there would be less surprise were it not that the city pokes up out of a vast expanse of prairie. There was a mist, and I couldn't tell whether the background to Denver was heavier mist or Rocky Mountains. I looked at the map in the American Automobile Association's useful guidebook and found that I had been deceived by a sort of optical illusion: because of Denver's tallness, I suppose, it appears to be in the middle of nowhere—but, in fact, the surrounding area is dotted with towns and villages. The names of some of those little places (Last Chance, for obvious instance) suggest that they sprang up in response to the gold or silver rushes—but why on earth is a town called Hygiene? North of Denver, two towns almost as close together as royal Windsor and academic Eton in Berkshire are called by those same names, except that the latter is misspelt "Eaton."

Understandably, none of the dozens of cabbies outside the station was willing to drive me the few blocks to my destination on my own, but a woman who looked elderly invited me to share her cab for the first part of her journey to a hospital where she was to receive specialist treatment for a chest complaint. She told me, "My doctor at home says the good air of Colorado will be the best medicine." Her voice was barely more than a whisper.

Very few of the too many hotels that describe themselves as being world famous really are—but the Brown Palace, which doesn't, deserves to. I had heard about it from several quarters before I learned that it was the scene of an interesting murder case. I had always assumed that Brown referred to the outside color of the building. Although that *is* brown, a booklet I received when I wrote to reserve a room informed me that the hotel is named after Henry C. Brown, a local tycoon who took over the construction when the two intending hoteliers, one an Englishman, ran out of cash even before the foundations were laid and opened *his* palace in 1892.

With the possible exception of the Taj Mahal, any exterior would seem drab compared with the interior of the Brown Palace. Eight stories of galleries—with intricate cast-iron railings, all painted sea green—surround an atrium that is roofed with stained glass. When the sun is high and unclouded, every gallery is tinctured with a lazy kaleidoscope of filtered colors. The entire floor of the atrium is covered with what looked to me like Persian carpets; glass screens make an avenue around the central square of the floor, which is the lounge, furnished with shiny tables, red-leather chairs and settees, and potted palms. Marble stairs, wide enough to require a banister at the center, lead up to a mezzanine beneath the lowest gallery, and little shops, all selling expensive things,

A recent picture of Denver's Brown Palace, as seen from the direction of the bar.

are tucked under the mezzanine. To the right of the entrance and the reception desk is one of three eating places; I think it was originally only a bar and has become a restaurant as well since 1911.

In my room-reserving letter I had said, without explanation, that I would like to stay in 404, 524, or 602, and it was 404 that I was given. As soon as I had glanced at the room, making sure that it had a bathroom (there wasn't one in 1911), I left the hotel and went, first of all, to the historical society, which, housed in a building that looks like a typewriter without keys, is as impressive as its counterpart in Chicago, and then, having been told by one of the NOBS in Cleveland that I mustn't miss it, to the Tattered Cover Book Store, which—large but sensibly sectioned, reminded me of Richard Booth's ex–cinema bookshop in Hay-on-Wye before that whole Welsh border town became a bibliopolic bazaar—I was glad not to have missed.

Then back to the Brown Palace, passing the gold-domed state capitol on the way. Another assumption proved to be wrong. I had thought that Denver's nickname, the Mile High City, was an exaggeration of the height of its skyscrapers, but the cabbie told me that the thirteenth step to the west entrance of the capitol is one mile above sea level. Wondering how that fact could be squared with the name of the hotel's bar-cum-restaurant, the Ship Tavern, I went in there and, sitting at the end of the counter nearer the wide-open windows, had my usual lunchtime drink, Dewar's White Label Scotch and ginger ale, and asked the red-haired barman to bring me a seafood salad, having determined to be calorie-conscious today. The salad whetted my appetite, and I didn't resist the barman's extolling of something called black-bottom pie, which turned out to be chocolate and custard in pastry, with cream on top, and chocolate on top of that.

I wandered into the lounge, where the harpist who plays there every afternoon had started playing. The Brown Palace has a historian, presently Corinne Hunt (who has written a book about the hotel). She joined me, and we talked about things that have happened there—mostly, of course, about what headline composers at the time, which was May 1911, called

THE DENVER SOCIETY MURDER

Actually, there were two murders—a fact that, though rarely adding to the interest as opposed to the intricacy of a case, gives a twist to the tale of this one. And there is something else that makes this case exceptional. Almost always, the reader of an account of a solved case that is new to him will soon know which character will turn out to be the murderer and which character is the *intended* victim. Correctly guessing readers apart, none will know which character played which role in the Denver case till a moment before the crime is committed.

John W. Springer, who was in his early fifties in 1911, was among the wealthiest citizens of Denver, which is saying something because lucky strikes of silver and gold in the nearby mountains and cattle raising on the surrounding prairies had resulted in a city that had more than its fair share of wealthy citizens. Springer had married into money, contentedly giving up a promising political career in his native state of Illinois to do so and, pooling the dowry with his less considerable assets, had vastly increased the capital by investing in local banks and development companies.

His wife died in 1904. A few years later, while doing business in St. Louis, he met Isabelle Patterson, a beautiful divorcée still in her twenties. He was instantly smitten. Somehow, his father-in-law learned that he intended to marry Isabelle and hired private detectives to investigate her past. Whatever the detectives' findings were, they were found in double-quick time and were so uncomplimentary that the father-in-law wrote to Springer that he should return to Denver at once, leaving Isabelle in St. Louis. But when Springer did return, his wife-to-be was with him. Shortly before the marriage, the father-in-law withdrew every penny of his financial support to Springer and soon afterward, showing how intensely he feared that the morals of his grandchildren would be marred by their association with the second Mrs. Springer, assumed custody of them, apparently without hindrance from their father, and took them to live in a place far distant from Denver.

There was, of course, an outbreak of tongue wagging in local society circles, but that soon subsided—chiefly, it seems, because there was nothing new to say about Isabelle Springer, who kept herself very much to herself when she was within gossip range of the city, which wasn't all that often, for, apparently without complaint from her husband, she left him as a grass-widower during the uncomfortably hot months of each year, spending them in Manhattan. (It subsequently emerged that her eastern evacuations were not only to prevent suntan, which was considered the poor's substitute for rouging in those days, but also to engage in activities described as bohemian. Drug taking was one; posing in scanty attire for "counterfeit Titians of the attics" was another. Presumably a newspaperman perceived a similarity between Isabelle's secret and amateur modeling and the modeling, nearly all publicized, that had gone a long way toward keeping Evelyn Nesbitt solvent till she became Mrs. Harry K. Thaw. I cannot think of a better reason behind the birth of a catchphrase, "The Thaw Case of the West," linking what happened in the Brown Palace in 1911 with Thaw's killing of Stanford White on the roof of Madison Square Garden five years earlier.)

Surprisingly, no gossip seems to have been sparked by the fact that, though John Springer possessed two residences, a just-out-of-town mansion on a ranch of twelve thousand acres and a fine house on Washington Street, a few blocks from the Brown Palace, Isabelle insisted that she also required a permanent suite on the sixth floor of the hotel. She lived as often there, apparently without the company of her husband, as she did at the places *he* treated as homes.

We have by now had enough "apparentlys" about Springer that they add up to *facts,* the clearest of those being that money was, to him, not the means to an end but the end itself—or rather, the means of making more money. When he spent (as opposed to invested) money, it was usually in what he considered the good cause of leaving himself free to increase his riches. He had made a mistake in marrying the beautiful Isabelle, but the mistake might well have been scaled down, though not rectified, if he had devoted less time to being a tycoon and more to being a husband—and if he had done so, several tragedies would almost certainly have been averted.

In the spring of 1911, round about the same week, two men came to Denver. One was a freelance business promoter named Frank Henwood, who was in his early thirties, dark, and spruce; he said that his home was in New York, but he does not seem to have mentioned that he had a wife and two children there. The purpose of his visit was to raise funds for a gas plant in Denver, and before long he interested John Springer in the venture. Within weeks of being introduced to Mrs. Springer, he was very friendly with her; she visited him in his room on the fifth floor of the Brown Palace, he visited her in her suite on the floor above, and he spent nights with her when she, alone, was at the mansion on the Springer ranch.

The other man who came to Denver, Tony Von Phul, was known throughout the country for his acts of daring as a balloonist; he held several height and distance records. He spoke openly of two reasons for his visit: to drum up financial support for the first flight over the nearby Pike's Peak and to tout for orders on behalf of a wine company. A native of St. Louis, he had known Isabelle—known her intimately in the biblical sense—before she left that city to marry John Springer, and he had met her during return trips she had made, at least till 1909. As soon as he arrived in Denver, booking into the Brown Palace, he renewed the acquaintance. He saw almost as much of her as did Frank Henwood. The latter, a year younger than Von Phul, was never more than formally polite to him—and by the middle of May public meetings between them, more often than not in the hotel bar, were noticeably unconvivial, almost always ended by one rudely walking away while the other was speaking.

For the continuation of the story till the crime, one can only go by testimony that was given at subsequent legal proceedings. Courtroom testimony rarely provides anything like the whole truth, and in this case, much of it lacks corroboration—which itself carries no guarantee of truthful support.

One reason for Henwood's unfriendliness toward Von Phul was that Isabelle had told him, presumably tearfully, that the balloonist had "some foolish little letters" that she had written to him years before and was threatening to show them to her husband unless she renewed the intimate relationship they had enjoyed in St. Louis. Henwood drafted a letter for her to write to Von Phul, but it seems that she sent a letter that she herself had composed.

At lunchtime on May 23, which was a Tuesday, Henwood tipped a bellboy to call Von Phul out of the bar, and the two men held a heated discussion in the lobby. They agreed to meet again at 5:30, but near that time Henwood learned that Von Phul had hurried off to the Daniels and Fisher department store. He himself hurried off to the store—with such speed that he arrived there to find Isabelle in one of the departments and Von Phul heading toward her. There was another discussion, even more heated, and Von Phul told Henwood, "I've a notion to spill you all over the place." Leaving Isabelle to get on with her shopping, they returned to the Brown Palace "to have it out" in Von Phul's room, which was number 404. That this discussion was as inconclusive as the previous ones is indicated by the fact that it ended with Von Phul whacking Henwood with a wooden shoetree and then pointing a revolver at him. Before retreating to his own room, Henwood commented: "Any man who carries a gun is a coward. I never carried one in my life."

Shortly afterward Von Phul dashed up the two flights of stairs to Isabelle's suite. He accused her of "letting Henwood come between them" and, when she said that wasn't true, struck her across the face. Adding to his rage, he noticed that a photograph of himself that had stood on a dresser had been replaced by two photographs of Henwood. When she explained that his portrait had been torn up by Henwood, he tore up those of Henwood and enclosed some of the pieces with a note, "Frankie Dear, you destroyed my picture and here is part of yours," which, as soon as he left the suite, he got a hotel servant to deliver to his rival's room.

By the time the note was delivered, Henwood was at police headquarters, where he exhibited a nasty bruise on his forehead that he said had been caused by one of Von Phul's shoetrees, claimed that he had been threatened with a revolver, said that the argument was over Mrs. Springer but that neither she nor her husband was to be publicly involved, prophesied a murder unless Von Phul was run out of town—and was told by the chief of police that no preventive action could be taken.

Ever since Von Phul had been allotted room 404, which had no bath, he had been waiting for a room with a bath to become vacant. On the Tuesday evening such a vacancy occurred, and without Von Phul's knowledge a maid was sent to 404 to transfer his things to Number 524. Finding a revolver on the floor, she took it downstairs and was told by the clerk to take it with the rest of Von Phul's belongings to his new room. When Von Phul learned that he had been given a room on the fifth floor, he demanded one on the sixth, preferably 602 or 603, which were on either side of Isabelle's suite. Told that though 602 was available, it had no bath, he said that, even so, that was the room he wanted. He went up to 524, where he was soon joined by a maid. He told her what had to be moved to 602—but, strangely, completely forgot about his revolver. Later that evening the maid sent to tidy 524 found the weapon under the pillow, and it was again taken down to the office. This time it was put in the safe.

Compounding the curiousness of the Curious Affair of the Forgotten Revolver, whoever stowed the weapon in the safe forgot about it as completely as had—and did—its owner.

On the Wednesday morning Isabelle got a nasty shock when she emerged from her suite—for, the moment she did, Von Phul materialized from the doorway of room 602, ran the few steps along the corridor, and, gripping her wrist, warned her that if he saw Henwood entering the suite, he would "come right in and fix him." She went back inside, where she scribbled a note to Henwood, telling him of Von Phul's threat and entreating him to "wash his hands of the whole matter," and sent it in the care of her maid to Henwood, who was at the office he had rented in town.

Later in the morning Henwood telephoned the chief of police and again pleaded with him to take action against Von Phul. The chief said that nothing could be done that did not risk unpleasant publicity for the Springers, and so Henwood hung up.

At about six in the evening Isabelle, having checked that Von Phul was not on sentry in his doorway, slipped down to Henwood's room and implored him to forget about her "foolish little letters." His reaction was to phone the chief of police and, having got through, try to persuade her to take over the call. Weeping, she ran out.

There were three theaters in the center of Denver. It would be apt if, on that Wednesday evening, one or some of the characters in the Henwood–Von Phul melodrama had sat through the melodrama of *East Lynne* at the Baker—but no: the Springers and Henwood went to the Orpheum, where a vaudeville program was headed by a Mademoiselle Bianci Froelich, a Russian performer of "classical and novelty dances," and Von Phul accompanied new acquaintances to the Broadway, facing the Brown Palace, to see Florenz Ziegfeld's touring *Follies,* which, as well as featuring Fanny Brice, was sometimes overcrowded by a seventy-five-strong bevy of showgirls.

It seems that John Springer had decided to spend the night in the suite; perhaps Isabelle, so muddled by fears about her new next-door neighbor that she felt that *any* man's nocturnal company would be better than none, had invented a different reason for pleading with her husband to stay. In any event, Henwood accompanied the Springers to the sixth floor, wished them goodnight, then went down to the bar. The

The Brown Palace Bar, ca. 1911. Courtesy Denver Public Library, Western Heritage Department.

time was about 11:15. Standing at the counter, he sipped a glass of wine, apparently abstracted, unaware of the twenty or so other customers.

A quarter of an hour later, Von Phul entered in the company of one of the *Follies* party. They too stood at the counter. At first Henwood and Von Phul were separated by the latter's acquaintance, but after a few minutes Von Phul changed places. He casually dipped his finger in Henwood's glass and stirred the wine. Henwood pretended not to notice. Von Phul said something. No one but Henwood heard the remark. Whatever it was, Henwood felt obliged to snap a reply. No one but Von Phul heard the words. Whatever they were, they so enraged him that, rather than continuing the exchange of unpleasantries, he directed an uppercut at Henwood's chin with such effect, more of surprise than force, that Henwood fell over backward.

Some of the other customers, their attention at last drawn to the contretemps at the counter, subsequently recalled that Von Phul immediately and contemptuously turned away from his fallen foe and indicated to the barman that both he and his *Follies* acquaintance required refills of their glasses. But other at last attentive customers subsequently recalled that he stood over the horizontal Henwood and put a hand on his hip, giving the impression that he was reaching for a gun holstered from his belt.

Henwood too—so he subsequently insisted—gathered that Von Phul was about to produce a gun, was about to shoot him with it. We know that, going by Henwood's account of one of the preceding incidents, he had told Von Phul: "Any man who carries a gun is a coward. I never carried one in my life"—seeming to imply that he had no intention of doing so. But if that implication is correct, he had had second thoughts: a few hours before the outing to the theater with the Springers—some time between his phone calls to the chief of police—Henwood had bought a .38 revolver. It had been stuck in his waistband ever since.

Now he sat up on the barroom floor and, presumably after some rummaging, produced the weapon, undid the safety catch, and fired at the man who was standing either over or with his back to him. Three of the six bullets hit different parts of the target. The first went through Von Phul's shoulder; as he ran toward the door, the second grazed his wrist; just as he reached the door, the third hit him in the groin, causing him to fall.

Two businessmen from the area of Colorado Springs, south of Denver, were injured by Henwood's errant shots. George Copeland, the owner of a samples-manufacturing firm, was hit twice below the knee. The remaining bullet went through the leg of a building contractor, James Atkinson, who, smoking a cigar at the time, kept it clenched between his teeth as he fell and continued to smoke it while lying on the floor.

Henwood got to his feet. Holding the emptied revolver by its muzzle, he strolled into the lobby, taking care not to step on Von Phul, and waited for the summoned police to arrive. The first person to assist Von Phul was a young musician, a member of the small orchestra that had just finished playing in the restaurant. Kneeling, he used Von Phul's hankie to stem the blood from the graze on his wrist, the least serious but presently only visible wound. The musician was Denver-born Paul Whiteman, who by the 1920s was the leader of the most popular dance band in the world.

Henwood was questioned at the police station, Von Phul less inten-sively at St. Luke's Hospital, to which he had traveled in a cab, having insisted that he would not be seen dead in an ambulance. Both men were amazingly chivalrous, each refusing to say an unkind word about the other (Von Phul described Henwood as a "good sport"; Henwood said that Von Phul's finger-in-the-wine provocation was simply the absentminded act of a connoisseur of wine)—and also refusing to ad-mit that "the woman in the case" was Isabelle Springer. Perhaps Von Phul would have become less chivalrous, as did Henwood, if he had not died the following morning. His death was followed a few days later by that of George Copeland, the samples manufacturer, after his wounds were infected with gangrene.

The district attorney may have felt that there was a reason of law for not charging Henwood with both of the murders, but there seems to be no satisfactory explanation as to why he decided that the single charge filed should relate to the murder of Copeland rather than that of Von Phul. It has been suggested that the DA, either friendly with or hopeful of favors from John Springer, wanted to keep the Isabelle motive out of the case, but that makes no sense at all: within days of the shootings it was common knowledge in Denver that they were the outcome of a feud concerning Isabelle—also that her husband was now suing for divorce. . . .

And she was the star prosecution witness at the trial. If Henwood hoped—or expected—that she would aid his defense by saying that he had acted entirely in response to her pleas in all his stormy dealings with Von Phul, he was disappointed. It was true, she said, that she had asked him to try to persuade Von Phul to return the "foolish little let-ters"—but though, almost at once, she had changed her mind, he had "continued to be an unwanted meddler. . . . I asked Mr. Henwood to stay out for my sake, for my husband's sake, and for the sake of my home."

The trial, lasting just over a week, ended on June 29, 1911, when the jury found Henwood guilty of murder in the second degree. Instead of waiting till the judge decided the sentence, which could be any term of imprisonment between ten years and life, Henwood made a long and very rude speech about him, saying that he was "a prosecuting judge" and accusing him of trying the case "on the merits of the Springer divorce suit." The speech may not have influenced the judge's sentencing decision, which was life imprisonment.

Henwood, who must have been either of considerable private means or the recipient of funds from a wealthy benefactor, lived like a lord in prison, having restaurant meals brought to him in his cozy cell while his lawyers fought for a retrial. They argued that the judge had misdirected the jury by ruling out the verdict of manslaughter—also, eventually, that because the statute of limitations meant that Henwood could never be charged with the death of Von Phul, he had in effect been cleared of that charge and therefore could not be considered guilty of the *ancillary* death of Copeland. Meanwhile John Springer's lawyers achieved their client's divorce from Isabelle, who was given fifteen thousand dollars and allowed to keep her jewels and her car.

After nearly two years of legal maneuvering, Henwood was granted a retrial. He was jubilant, convinced that his acquittal was a foregone conclusion. Isabelle's letters to Von Phul, which had been excluded at the first trial, were read aloud—causing much oohing among the spectators, for some passages sounded lustful as well as loving. John Springer, called by the defense, said that Henwood was "always a gentleman" and added, "I never saw anything improper in his attitude towards Mrs. Springer."

The case went to the jury on June 17, 1913. After deliberating for seven hours, they returned a different verdict: Henwood was guilty of murder in the *first* degree. He was sentenced to death.

Shortly before the execution was scheduled, the governor of Colorado commuted the sentence to life imprisonment with hard labor. In 1922, after Henwood had been in jail for nine less cosseted years than the two he had already served, he received a parole from a different governor. His freedom was short-lived. A few months after his release, while living in Mexico under an assumed name, he threatened to murder a young woman unless she agreed to marry him, and his novel idea of what constituted a shotgun marriage led to his being returned to a Colorado prison as a parole violator. He died there in 1929. Although George Copeland's wounds in the leg had not in themselves been particularly serious, he had died as the result of them. It appears that Frank Henwood died somewhat similarly, from infection to the slight surgical wound of an operation on his tonsils.

He outlived Isabelle by a dozen years. Following her divorce and before Henwood's retrial, she moved to Manhattan. Both the cash payment and the proceeds from the sale of the disposable items of the divorce settlement were soon spent, chiefly on drugs. She used the loveliness of her face and form to obtain money, at first as a bit player in cheap movies, then as an artist's model, then also as a prostitute; but when her addiction decayed her beauty and made her old beyond her years, she was left with no means of livelihood. If she gave her true age when she was taken to the paupers' hospital on Blackwell's Island, she was thirty-six in the spring of 1917, which was when she died there.

As it was one of the afternoons when Corinne Hunt takes sightseers around the Brown Palace, she couldn't sit and talk with me for as long as I should have liked. I asked the waiter what I might expect if I ordered tea, and he grinned, saying that he was used to English guests asking that question and assured me that the pot would, of course, be warmed, the tea *then* put into it, and boiling water *then* poured onto it. And so I ordered some. Usually when one asks for tea in America, one is given a cupful of water, barely hot enough to produce steam, and a teabag, more bag than tea, to swizzle in it; by the time the water becomes muddily discolored, it is tepid.

While enjoying the good tea, I listened to the harp music. Harps make a nice noise, but it is so ornate that I can rarely make out the melody. At one point the harpist played what I thought I recognized as "Greensleeves," and I only realized that I must have been wrong when she announced that she was about to play "Greensleeves." (I've just thought that I can't remember ever seeing a *man* playing a harp, not even in Wales, and I wonder whether any other musical instrument is so sexist.)

It was about four o'clock when I left the hotel and wandered around the shopping district. A red London bus, permanently parked, is used as a booking office for entertainments. I have seen any number of these buses in America, and I shouldn't be surprised if before long there are more over here then there are left in London, where, for a reason that must be daft, many of the red double-deckers are being replaced by buses of other shapes, sizes, and colors. Partly likewise, many of London's "*black* cabs" are now painted garishly—some to the shocking extent of pink, for the shameful reason that they are also itinerant placards for the blush-colored *Financial Times;* yet others, advertising the Yellow Pages books of advertisements, look almost as lovely as massive dollops of vomit. London, once a colorful city, is turning dull from the addition of more colors than a rainbow.

I traipsed around the central Denver shops without buying anything (and without finding the Daniels and Fisher department store, which must have been taken over or gone bust), then strolled south to a Wild Western sort of restaurant called the Buckhorn Exchange, where I had an early, and excellent, dinner. The chatty waiter said that I should have my steak cooked "no more than a short distance from rare—don't want to kill it a second time, right?" and I was glad that I followed his advice. He was so chatty that I quite forgot to ask him how the place had got its name. He told me, among other things, that it "laid claim to being" the oldest restaurant in Denver, having "opened its portals" in the 1890s; that it was the "proud possessor" of Colorado Liquor License No. 1; and that the "muriels" outside had been painted by redskins in exchange for meals. (I have never seen any red Indians but hope to when I get farther west. I wonder if they have been asked what they think of the idea that they ought to be called "Native Americans"—and what other Americans born in America think of their exclusion from that category. I am convinced that the game played by English children when I was one of them would never have caught on if it had been called "cowboys and Native Americans"; but I suppose the same applies to the once equally enjoyed game if it had been called "doctors and neonatal nurse practitioners.")

When I got back, feeling tired, to the Brown Palace, the harpist had finished her stint and a pianist had taken over, playing all sorts of pieces, a classical number one minute, a popular tune the next. After a while, probably more to relieve his aching bum than from a desire for audience participation, he wandered to nearby tables, requesting requests. I doubt if any hotel pianist ever does that without being asked for "As Time Goes By." I didn't really want a drink, but I ordered one to save the small embarrassment from monopolizing an empty table while listening to the music.

I shouldn't have ordered it—or rather, shouldn't have drunk all of it, as American drinks from the bar are a lot more generous than those served in England—and by the time I got up to room 404 I could scarcely keep my eyes open. I reluctantly took a bath, only because I vaguely foresaw the unlikelihood of my being able to sit out of sniffing distance of people for the next couple of days, haphazardly packed my big bag, phoned room service for a wake-up call in the morning, and, though I had given my teeth a trivial brush, ate the chocolate mints that the chambermaid, or whatever she is called over here, had left on my pillow. I don't remember flopping into bed and switching off the light, but I must have done.

Slowly to Oakland

A mtrak's timetables also show the distance between stops, and if my arithmetic is right, Oakland is about fourteen hundred miles from Denver. Again if my arithmetic is right, the journey is supposed to take thirty-three hours: from nine in the morning till five in the afternoon of the following day (there is an extra hour because of the change from Mountain to Pacific Time at the border between Utah and Nevada). I had felt uneasy about this part of my trip since, a few months ago, I tried to book a sleeper and was told that I was several months too late. Perhaps if all had gone well with the locomotive, my uneasiness would have proved to be as overgloomy as uneasinesses usually are; indeed, the uneasiness would probably have worked like a preventive medicine, for as the actual discomforts would not have seemed half as bad as I expected them to be, I might hardly have noticed them. The trouble was that all did not go well with the locomotive.

The first, before-lunch part of the journey passed in what seemed like no time at all. West of Denver, the many-colored prairies are suddenly halted by the Rockies. The train travels through canyons so high that, from my aisle seat, I couldn't see the tops of them; the sides, often almost vertical, are covered with massive natural sculptures that, as one stares at them, seem to change shape, sometimes becoming recognizable as Mount Rushmore–like faces, animals, or manmade things such as staircases and skyscrapers.

I wished that I could check whether what I recognized was apparent to the old lady sitting next to me, but she rarely glanced through the window and took no notice when I spoke to her.

Later on I suddenly realized that she was deaf—and, political correctness being so dreadfully pervasive, instantly wondered whether "deaf" was on the increasingly lengthened list of banned words, replaced by some cockeyed term coined, or rather counterfeited, by a fanatic with a tin ear—"auditorily challenged," perhaps. I myself have some d-blank-blank-fness in one ear; and so, but far more so, does Dean Keller's wife, Pat (who I am quite certain, for she is wonderfully sensible, does not want her hereditary disorder renamed). Oh, how I despise euphemisms—for several reasons, one being that they often muddy meanings. Years ago, long before the outbreak of PC, I was among a group of theater people who traveled to a convent near Liverpool, hoping to cheer up some at-least-octogenarian nuns. By the time we found the place, one of our number, a brilliant but disheveled pianist named Ronnie Settle, was dying for a pee—but, not knowing how to put that to the welcoming Mother Superior, he enquired, ever so genteelly, if he might wash his hands. She said, "But of course, my son," and sailed off through a doorway, only to return shortly afterward, laden with a bucket of steaming water, an unwrapped bar of pink Camay soap, and a striped bath towel. I cannot remember the sequel to her reappearance, which affected the bladders of the rest of us, but I have an idea that Ronnie Settle decided that he had no choice but to make a mess where he agonizingly stood. If that little tale doesn't have a moral, I'm blessed if I know which does.

The deaf (I insist) old lady was only an inch or so taller than my next-seat neighbor from Cleveland to Chicago. She also was a knitter, but not mystifyingly: I could tell that she was making a jumper for a baby or a midget. Rather than knitting nonstop, she worked in spells of about an hour, then either took a nap or read a paperback, a romance novel by Barbara Cartland (whom I *heard* recently, though only just, on a record of her singing-saying sentimental songs, accompanied by the Royal Philharmonic Orchestra and a choir, both so subdued—else she would not be heard at all—as to make me think that she could have managed quite as well with a three-piece band—piano, piano player, and piano stool—and a pair of those pathetic singers who are hired to make "didum, didum" noises whenever the star is taking breaths or has forgotten the words). Not once throughout the journey did I see the elderly knitting-napping-reading lady eat or drink anything, and I never needed to rearrange my legs so that she could get past to go to a lavatory, the restaurant, or the café. She must have done at least one of the things I didn't see her do while I was away, which was quite often—usually in the café, there always to smoke a cigarette and sometimes for a drink.

On one of my first visits to the café, I sat opposite a man whom I took to be in his thirties. I wondered, on account of his quaint mixture of old casual clothes, if he were a fare-paying hobo. I cannot have disguised my interest in his clothes, for he said, surprising me by the good quality of his voice, "No point in dressing up for what I'm doing for the next couple of weeks"—fishing in a tributary of the Colorado River. He said that there was no better medicine than "fishing without caring about catching anything." He did it, usually in the same stretch of river, whenever he could get away from his work as a political journalist in Massachusetts, writing a column under the byline of Politicus that was syndicated to many newspapers in the state. His name was David Mittell.

Our conversation was interrupted by a man who sat beside me before asking, "Mind if I sit here?" He was sure that we would be amazed to hear that he was eighty-two. He was on his way to "take a peek" at his newest great-grandchildren, who—he was sure we would be amazed to hear—were triplets: "three of them, would you believe?" He then launched into a patter of jokes, most of them the sort one finds in Christmas crackers, the others a trifle risqué (a fact that he indicated to me, the Innocent Englishman Abroad, by nudging my arm at each punch line, twice causing me to spill my drink), and, having exhausted his repertoire or concluded that neither of his audience had a sense of humor, abruptly got up, saying, "See you round like an orange," and pottered off in search of others to pester.

I was watching to make sure that he really had gone when David Mittell said, "Look, there's a buffalo." But just as I turned back and looked through the window, the train entered one of the many tunnels through the mountains. Mittell spoke angrily of "scientific criminals" who had crossed a buffalo with a cow to make "a more useful creature" they call a beefalo.

He left shortly afterward, because the train was approaching his stop, Glenwood Springs. Wyatt Earp's crony, the psychopathic dentist John "Doc" Holliday, died in a tuberculosis sanitarium there in 1887. It is said that his last words were "I'll be damned," expressing surprise that he was dying with his boots *off.*

On a subsequent visit to the café I met a slightly built, heavily mustached Latin American. His name (he wrote it on a paper napkin for me) was Nuevo Espinoza. He was a born-again Christian. During the most recent of many terms of imprisonment for drug-related crimes, he had suddenly Seen the Light; on his release he had persuaded the owner of a dilapidated property in Fresno to allow him to turn it into a halfway house, a place where young paroled prisoners could live for periods of up to about six months, he meanwhile trying to help them, practically as well as spiritually, to "stay straight"; he, all on his own, had made the house habitable, using tools and decorating materials that he had cadged and furniture that had been thrown away, and had then "welcomed the first party of residents to 'New Hope.'" That, I gathered, was five or six years ago. He now received funds from charitable organizations, and some local businesses helped both financially and by accepting residents for employment, "no questions asked about the past." I expressed admiration at what he had done, was doing, but he refused to take any credit, saying that he "worked gratefully for the Lord." He shrugged when I asked how many of his residents had stayed straight. "One in ten," I suggested, and he said, "Well, maybe that many."

Later he said: "Drugs, that's the letter-A, number-one problem—don't I know it, speaking for myself. They make two crimes in one, maybe more than two: using drugs, that's one crime; getting the money to pay for them, that makes another. And another. Keep counting." I told him what I thought: that, as there is no solution to the drug problem, it would be worth seeing what happened if drugs were made legal and addicts could get what they needed on prescription. That would greatly reduce the drug-dealers' profits, would put some of them out of business. And there would be far fewer crimes committed for the sole purpose of obtaining money to buy drugs. Nuevo Espinoza, a very polite man, said that maybe, just maybe, there was something in the idea.

Not wanting the night to seem longer than I dreaded it was going to seem, I waited till the last sitting of dinner. When I would have been eating the cheese, had the triangle of cheese been eatable (the description, *French* Cheddar, on the label should have warned me not to waste ten minutes prizing the silver paper open), the train came to a halt. It remained halted for an hour and a half.

Near the start of that interminable time, I went back to my seat, noticing with envy that nearly every passenger was already sound asleep. I have never, when trying to sleep sitting up, been able to; I know that I shall never master that simple knack, and as the knowledge makes a self-fulfilling prophecy, the knack will always elude me.

None of the sleepers was awoken by the peculiar explanation for the halt that boomed over the loudspeakers: the locomotive had run out of oil. I thought that was the end of the message, that of course there were spare cans of oil on board, but the voice went on to say that the oil had to be brought from the nearest station, which was called Helper. That name, presently apt, belongs to a little place in Utah where "helper locomotives" are added to eastbound freight trains, some of more than a hundred wagons, that single locomotives are not strong enough to pull over the mountains.

Hours that seemed like days after the oiling, sometime between two and three, we reached Salt Lake City, where we should have arrived between eleven and midnight. We stayed there for an hour or so. All I could see through the window was a trackside warehouse—of beds, I suppose, as the sign that stared at me, sneered at me, said PERFECT SLEEPER.

Because of the café-only constraint on smoking, I had smoked fewer cigarettes during the day than I usually do—but during the night, more for respite from the misery of just sitting in a seat in the near darkness than because I felt like smoking, I made many trips to the café, which must have resulted in my doubling the number of cigarettes I had ever smoked within a period of twenty-four hours.

As Amtrak employs only one café attendant per train, and he needs time off for sleep, there is no café-service from midnight till six in the morning. Heaven knows why Amtrak hasn't installed drink machines;

surely it isn't for the fastidious reason that the stuff that comes out of them usually tastes like a mixture of the drinks that are supposed to come out separately. In the small hours even a connoisseur of hot drinks would prefer a plastic cup of something, or some things, to nothing at all. Whenever I visited the café, other people, not all of them smokers, were there; some I saw several times, and we smiled at one another in fellowship, as if we were members of a club we had been compelled to join.

At last, at long last, morning came: a false dawn, then the real thing. If my eyes had not felt as if they had been sandpapered, I would have been amazed by the sunrise—at first, straggles of navy blue and orange, blueberry purple where they overlapped—but I was simply relieved that the night was being wiped away. I washed and shaved, and feeling better than I was willing to admit to myself, went for breakfast.

I had noticed during the night, after Salt Lake City, that the train was rarely traveling at more than an amble, and my gloomy suspicion that, far from making up any of the lost time, we had lost more was confirmed when we got to Winnemucca, Nevada, shortly before ten rather than shortly after six. I read in the route guide that the little place was named after an Indian chief, "the Napoleon of the Paiutes," a tribe I had never heard of, and that Butch Cassidy and his gang had robbed the local bank, "trying to cash in on some of the profits from the gold, copper, and silver mines."

Half an hour after leaving Winnemucca, the train, still dawdling, entered an area of entire whiteness—a dried alkali lake, I heard someone say—and came to a halt. Without trying to imagine it, I imagined that the train wasn't a train at all but a ship stuck in an ice field; and, I suppose because lack of sleep was making me slightly delirious, I remembered a once-popular play, *Outward Bound,* in which the passengers on a ship gradually realize that they have died and are on the way to purgatory, and I decided that I didn't mind if purgatory was my destination as long as there were no further delays in getting there.

After a while, an apology for a "slight problem" crackled through the loudspeaker. An hour later, give or take a day or so, we heard that the problem was solved: the mechanic had discovered that bare wires hanging from the locomotive were touching the rails, causing short circuits. Eventually the train started ambling again.

At breakfast I had sat next to a Dublin neurologist whose rather military bearing and only slightly Irish voice seemed tailored to his name, Hugh Staunton, which he didn't seem to mind my saying sounded like that of a good-guy character in a Bulldog Drummond tale; he and his wife, who had not wanted breakfast, were traveling through western states after he had attended a conference in Vancouver.

Near lunchtime he sought me out and suggested drinks, and we went to the café, sitting in the nonsmoking part, where all the tables were empty. The train stopped at Reno. I had hoped to see a red Indian during my travels; but when I did, I wished I hadn't. He was just below our window, which faced the station buildings. He was drugged, or drunk, or both, and he was trying to tear the handbag from a chubby young woman wearing rainbow-colored, knee-length shorts and a T-shirt printed with pictures of James Dean. We could see, but could not hear, that she was screaming. There were many people close by, some had just got off the train, others were queuing to get on, but none was taking any notice. But then—no more than seconds after we first saw what was happening—a man went to help her. He was crippled in one leg, and when he got close, he hopped about on the good one and used his crutch like a spear, prodding at the Indian. Hugh Staunton and I automatically, unthinkingly, assumed that we were required to help.

Easier said than done. We hurried up the steps from the café, pushed through the crowded observation car, and found that the steps to the exit were clogged with people who had just got on the train. None of them voluntarily turned sideways on to let us through, and some of the men complained as we shoved past. By the time we got out, the Indian was shambling away; the woman had not let go of her bag. She thanked her rescuer. We spoke to him. "Just as well I've got a crocked leg," he said, still panting, "otherwise I wouldn't have had a kind of weapon, and I don't suppose I would have interfered." I didn't believe the last bit.

As Hugh Staunton and I walked back through the observation car to the café, a young, able-bodied man—we must have shoved past him on the steps—commented, "Really great to meet polite guys like you." We didn't reply. I ordered fresh drinks. Hugh Staunton said: "So many men who could have helped—should have helped. 'Don't get involved'—that's beginning to be the accepted advice in Dublin as well as over here; in British cities too, I believe."

Not changing the subject, I suggested that *some* well-intended publicity had an adverse effect, and I mentioned a recent study that indicated that a very expensive advertising campaign on English television that sought to deter youngsters from trying drugs had been followed, virtually at once, by an increase in the number of juvenile drug users. And then, now clearly to the point, I spoke of the Kitty Genovese case:

Shortly after three o'clock on the morning of March 13, 1964, a Friday, she drove her red Fiat into the parking area beside the Kew Gardens railway station in a pleasant part of the New York borough of Queens (four or five miles west of where Albert and Ruth Snyder once lived). She had driven from the bar she managed. She was fewer than fifty yards from her home, an apartment in a Tudorbethan block. She was twenty-eight; unmarried, for she was a lesbian. A snap of her, the only one that seems to have been published, shows that she was of less than medium height, slim, and had very dark hair, which she wore in a short, casual style that was then, perhaps still is, called an urchin cut.

She had walked only a few steps from her car, was on the curb in front of the Austin Book Shop in a row of shops next to the station forecourt, when she was attacked by a man with a knife. Her cries for help seemed to have frightened the man away—not far away, however, for as she staggered back the way she had come, he returned and stabbed her again, several times, and sexually molested her. Still crying out for help, she dragged herself to the entrance to a lane leading to the main road. There the man attacked her again. He had gone by the time a woman came from one of the nearby blocks and, finding Kitty Genovese dying, ran back to get a neighbor to phone the police. (Within a week a young black man named Winston Moseley, who was married and employed as a machine operator, was arrested for the crime; he confessed to it, saying that he had chanced on his victim "while cruising around, planning to rape and to rob and to kill a girl." He was sentenced to life imprisonment but escaped and committed further heinous crimes before being recaptured. It is to be hoped that he will not be allowed to escape again—and that his life imprisonment will be ended for no reason other than his death.)

Those last sentences are in brackets because Winston Moseley is immaterial to the fame of the case. And so, in a way, is Kitty Genovese.

At first, in the day or two following the crime, the New York papers took little notice of it; the report in the *Times* was of a half-dozen sentences, tucked away on an inside page. But then a *Times* journalist had lunch with a senior policeman, who spoke dispiritedly of matters associated with the murder at Kew Gardens—and soon afterward those matters became front-page news, were made the subject of an editorial. The Kitty Genovese case was transmuted into the Case of the Silent Witnesses. Thirty-eight of them, according to the *Times*'s count: residents in apartments close to one or another of the places where the girl had been attacked. They had heard her cries—some had even looked out of their windows and seen what was happening—but none had helped her, not even by phoning the police.

The *Times* "regretfully admitted" that it could not explain "such shocking indifference" but apparently assumed that the indifference *displayed* by people living in a very small part of Kew Gardens was *felt* by just about everyone else, for it asked, "What kind of people are we?" The story was taken up by other organs of the news media, not only in New York but also throughout the country; in England too—where, at that time, we *knew* that we could enjoy being smug in the knowledge that "such a thing could never happen here."

A couple of days before I set off on this Amtrak trip, Jeffrey Bloomfield, one of the friends I was staying with in Flushing, took me out to Kew Gardens. Speaking only of the look of the buildings and open spaces, the area seemed hardly to have altered since 1964. A pleasant place: not as pleasant as the namesake place near my home—but then, few other places in London are as pleasant as that. Learning that the Austin Book Shop had been moved to larger premises not far away, we walked there. It is in the area called Richmond Hill, which is not at all pleasant; no part that I saw (never far from the main Jamaica Avenue, which must be one of the few streets in New York still shaded by elevated-railway tracks that remain in use) was less grim than even the tattiest parts of the so-called deprived areas of London; the difference between this Richmond Hill and the one beside the Thames, a stroll from London's Kew Gardens, seemed to me to be dreadfully, inexcusably, extreme.

But now the Austin Book Shop is there. It is the best secondhand bookshop I have been in for many years. The owner, Bernard Titowsky— a bear of a man, made to look larger because he was wearing one of his giveaway "BOOK BUM" T-shirts that was several sizes too small for him— had a knowledge of books that can only have come from a love of them.*

He pouted when we mentioned Kitty Genovese. "Not that non-story again," he complained. But later, mellowed, he recalled arriving at his lockup shop in Kew Gardens a few hours after the crime, knowing nothing about it, and finding blood near the door. "I didn't know I was looking at blood—didn't take a brush to it. I guess time and rain washed most of it away."

I asked what he had meant by "non-story," and he said: "Thirty-eight—thirty-eight 'silent witnesses.' Don't ask me how the press came up with that very exact number. If it came from the police, some reporter ought to have known that cops aren't exactly noted for being geniuses at arithmetic. Maybe a few local people—but no more than a few—guessed that what was going on was more than the usual night-time ruckus. A few. No more than that."

He explained that, at the time, there was "a really bad bar" near the railway station; *every* night, people living in the area were awoken, kept awake, by the noise of drunks leaving the bar; often there were fights outside. Calls to the police had rarely been answered; on a few occasions a patrol car had arrived, but always so long after the call that the drunks had gone. According to Bernard Titowsky, "The real story of that night was the god-awful example of the cry-wolf thing." I am sure that he was speaking honestly, but honesty isn't necessarily truthfulness. Perhaps the truth of how many silent witnesses there were is somewhere between his "few" and the reporters' thirty-eight.

I am not questioning the honesty of a single one of the reporters when I say that Bernard Titowsky's cry-wolf explanation for the silence of most of the witnesses would not have made a story worthy of a lead position in so many papers and on so many television and wireless news programs. I am prepared to accept that the editors who gave prominence to the other story believed that they were acting for the public good. But I wonder whether such coverage of the story, rather than

*Bernard Titowsky has since died; his bookshop remains.

shocking all of those readers, viewers, and listeners who were expected to be shocked, caused some of them to think that the very fact that the silent witnesses in Kew Gardens were ordinary, decent people meant that noninvolvement had become unexceptional. *Some* news stories must influence public attitudes—and some of those stories must affect behavior. Assuming that some contributed toward what is now the widespread belief that it is only natural to pretend unawareness of a criminal act (there were far more than thirty-eight silent witnesses to the attempted theft at Reno Station), I doubt that any was more influential then the one that made scant reference to a girl named Kitty Genovese.

In the early afternoon, unable to think of a less useless way of whiling away some of the time till Oakland and in the Panglossian hope that I had come up with an improved variation on sedative sheep-counting, I counted the Richmonds in the state-by-state index to my Rand McNally Atlas, and when I got to the little list for Wyoming, which doesn't have any, had reached twenty-five. I tried, though not hard, to remember how many American Manchesters I had counted when, years ago, the English Manchester's *Evening News* asked me to write a series about some of them. I couldn't remember the number—more than a dozen—but recalled my surprise that, in looking for Manchesters, I spotted an excess of ladylike-sounding Marions. I had found enough material for the series on American Manchesters in a convenient two of them, one in New Hampshire, the other, a lovely place, on the coast of Massachusetts. After discarding the idea of recounting the Manchesters, I quite impressed myself by remembering that the name Richmond means "strong (enough for a fort) hill" and that the "chester" part of the Lancastrian Manchester shows that the city grew from a Roman fort.

At teatime, when the train should have just left California's Richmond, the last stop before Oakland, it was somewhere between Truckee and Colfax, the first two stops in California. I can be more exact than that. The train was zigzagging along shelves cut into the high slopes of the Sierras, where there are still some of the original wooden tunnels protecting the track from the heavy snowfalls of winter.

I was tetchy as well as tired because my tiredness had misted my eyes to the glories of the surroundings. I had rubbed my eyes so as to be sure of seeing Donner Lake, which is named after the leaders of a party of more than eighty settlers from the East that became stranded amid house-high falls of snow near the lake in the winter of 1846. Weeks after leaving the main party, some members of a small "Forlorn Hope" group reached help, and a rescue team was sent to the lake; forty of the trapped settlers had survived, but only by feeding from the flesh of the dead.

Somewhere near Sacramento, the state capital, a roly-poly conductor sought to entertain us over the loudspeakers. I couldn't make out whether he fancied himself as a singer or as an impressionist. Whichever, the audience response was more entertaining than the entertainment. He began with an approximation of Al Jolson singing "California, Here I Come," which, as well as prompting naughty shouts on the subject of orgasm, caused a woman with surprisingly purple hair to remark: "Say, will someone tell that poor lost guy that—sure, it's hard to believe—but we CAME to California some miles back." Undeterred, the conductor regaled us with the Tony Bennett version of "I Left My Heart in San Francisco," complete with the orchestral diddle-diddle-dee / diddle-diddle-dum bits. That was greeted with raspberries, and I was concerned to hear the elderly man across the aisle muttering to his wife that, supposing we ever *got* to San Francisco, he might really need to leave his heart there; he cannot have been encouraged by her reply, that she didn't think a fourth heart bypass was possible.

I had expected cheers—had intended joining in with them—when the train arrived at Oakland Station. But there was no show of relief, audible or visible, when it did arrive—well after nine o'clock, more than four hours late. The last message over the loudspeakers had warned passengers not to leave the station on foot, and everyone had seemed to know the reason for the warning: that the proximate part of Oakland, virtually taken over by drug addicts and peddlers, has become known as the Murder Capital of America—far more disquieting than Cleveland's boast of being the Car-Theft Capital of the World. (I must say, though, that there does seem to be rather a lot of self-proclaimed Murder Capitals in this country—suggesting rivalry between various police forces, each masochistically keen to bump up its homicide statistics so as to claim outright victory as the best loser in the fight against crime.)

Mercifully, a fleet of Amtrak *buses* was waiting in the fenced forecourt. They took us across the Bay Bridge to San Francisco, to a depot, where, again mercifully, there were plenty of cabs, one of which took me to my hotel, the St. Francis.

I had fretted that, during the hours since I was supposed to have checked in, my reservation would have been cancelled; but all was well. My room, on the ninth floor, nice and close to a lift, was palatial. The bellboy said that I looked as if I needed a drink, and I said that, in that case, I had better have a Dewar's White Label with Schweppes ginger ale; also, as long as the kitchen had English mustard (other sorts are no more mustard than French cheddar is Cheddar), a plain beef sandwich. He used one of the phones. One of them. There were, inexplicably, four. A minute or so after I had undressed and put on a complimentary bathrobe, the drink and sandwich, exactly what I had asked for, were delivered.

I set the tray on the lavatory lid, got into an excessively bubbly bath, and after savoring the experience, new to me, of feeling like Claudette Colbert as Cleopatra, used the adjacent phone to call an old friend, George Raine, a brilliant journalist who now works for the *San Francisco Examiner,* to explain why I hadn't phoned earlier, to thank him for the things in an envelope that he had left at the mail counter downstairs, and to find out where I was to meet him and his wife, Kay, the following night. When I boasted that I was phoning from the bath, he said that he had always thought that hotel bathside phones were meant for SOS calls and knowingly misquoted the only line of Stevie Smith's poetry that anyone remembers, saying, "I'm not bathing but drowning."

A few minutes later, having, among other things, drunk every last dribble of the scotch and eaten every crumb of the sandwich, I was in bed—not wearing pajamas because I wanted the delight from the touch of cool, crisp sheets to be entire—and within seconds was sound asleep.

I rarely remember dreams. But because the dream I awoke from (the only time I awoke throughout the night) was, as it were, the opposite of a dream, it couldn't possibly be forgotten. It was about being on the train from Denver, about being *unable* to sleep; I even felt the twinges and cricks and cramps from almost continuous sitting. Awakening from the dream of being awake, I was fuddled into believing that the dream was the reality, that *now* I was dreaming. I hoped that, having at last fallen asleep on the train, I would sleep till Oakland, all the time dreaming about being in bed.

In San Francisco

I woke up, and straightway got up, at seven. At first, still tipsy from sleep, I knew that I had to be up that early but couldn't think why. It wasn't till I was in the bathroom, had not merely doused but had clouted my face with cold water, that I knew the reason—*Alcatraz*. The envelope that George Raine had left for me contained a ticket across to the island: the first ferry of the day, at nine o'clock. I had asked him to get the ticket, having read that it was necessary to book.

I left the hotel and had coffee and an English muffin while standing in a café on Mason Street. (English muffins, ubiquitous in America, are practically unobtainable in England. They truly ring bells in my mind, for one of my earliest memories is of the jingle-jangle of the bells rung by muffin-men, trays hanging on strings round their necks, who touted in suburban streets before teatime on Sundays. If muffins ever make a comeback in England, I expect they will be marketed as American muffins.)

The weather was perfect, like that of a fine autumn morning at home, and though some of the ups in the corrugations of the land toward Fisherman's Wharf made me pant, I was not at all sweaty when I got to Pier 41. Hopelessly intemperate when it comes to mementoes, I bought too many overpriced and useless things in the ferryside gift shop and, embarrassed by the glossy white-and-black carrier bag that said "I SPENT TIME ON ALCATRAZ," joined the already long queue of ticket holders waiting to be allowed on the ferry.

One of the two exquisite young men in front of me said to the other, "I suppose Alcatraz is named after Al Capone," and the other replied, "Well, yes, I guess so, honey." Believing that, with couples like that, two's company but a third butting in is liable to get his face scratched, I didn't tell them what I had just learned from a guidebook, that the island was called *Isla de Alcatraces*—Island of Pelicans—by Spanish sailors who explored the bay in the eighteenth century. After being used as a fortress, then as a military prison, Alcatraz became a federal penitentiary for "incorrigible or disruptive prisoners," opening as such in 1934.

Capone was among the first arrivals, transferred from Atlanta, where for the previous two years, since beginning his sentence for tax evasion, he had lived the life of Riley and had continued to control his business interests in and away from Chicago. He remained "on the rock" for four and a half years, during which time he was diagnosed as having incurable syphilis. He served the rest of his sentence (which, with time off for good behavior, lasted till the end of 1939) in far less punitive places and was then taken to his home in Florida, where he lived, a virtual recluse, till his death in January 1947.

On the ferry across to the island, a trip of ten minutes or so, I wondered what made a visit to a disused prison the leading tourist attraction in San Francisco. Many of the passengers had babies in arms or in pushchairs; many were eating odorous things they had bought at fast-food kiosks on the wharf (which must have explained the swarms of flies). I wondered without loftiness, for my own reason for visiting Alcatraz was inadequate—simply because not visiting the place during a "murder tour" would seem a blatant omission. The only other prison-for-tourists I had visited was at Bodmin in Cornwall: far older than this one, far longer disused. Perhaps because of an inherent chilliness in one of the decrepit buildings, I had had an attack of the shivers there; I had learned afterward that it was the execution shed.

Alcatraz ceased to be a prison in 1963. Six years later militant Indians occupied the island, claiming it as the "Home of Free Indians" (the

On the ferry to Alcatraz.

slogans they daubed on walls and on the watertank have not been erased). The authorities allowed the occupation to continue for a year and a half—till the summer of 1971, when U.S. marshals landed and took the few remaining Indians into custody. The island is now administered by the National Park Service.

As soon as everyone was off the ferry, a park ranger gave a jokey talk that included some statistics: though there were 336 cells, there were never more than 302 prisoners; there were eight murders, five suicides, and no executions; of 39 prisoners who attempted to escape, 7 were shot dead, 6 definitely drowned in the bay, and 5 who were never captured and never heard of again are presumed to have drowned. The ranger pointed out that Robert Stroud, the double-murderer who was portrayed by Burt Lancaster as a charming old fellow in a movie, *Birdman of Alcatraz*, showed no interest in birds during the seventeen years he spent on the island, from 1942; his ornithological research, which he seems to have taken up so as to obtain alcohol, ostensibly for experiments, was confined to the earlier years he had spent in Leavenworth.

Since that movie appeared, at about the time of the closure of the island prison, one can hardly switch on a television set, in this country or in mine, without finding a "drama documentary," usually publicized as being based on true criminous events and always leaving the poor lay viewer entirely in the dark as to which bits of it are somewhere near factual, which bits are wholly fictional. I once suggested to a TV executive that it would be helpful to unwary viewers—and, warming to my theme, more honest, supposing that honesty mattered to him— if the truthful ingredients of such programs were shown in black and white, the untruthful ones in color—and added, my warmth now up to boiling point, that he would not need to spend more than a pittance on monochrome processing. And recently, sparked by a pack-of-lies "true movie," I wrote a letter that was published in the *London Daily Telegraph,* reading in part: "Virtually all of the current spate of televised 'true-crime dramas' are littered with designed inaccuracies and complete inventions. Heaven knows why I, a crime historian, was hired to provide facts about certain murder cases to be used in a recently shown series. The concoctors of the scripts wrote what they pleased, regardless of the truth. Years ago, already despairing, I noted that legend is more pliable, and therefore more durable, than truth. It is surely worrying that millions of viewers are deceived into believing that these 'true crime' programmes present the truth, the whole truth, and nothing but the truth. In this context, dramatic license is dramatic perjury."

Inside Alcatraz I strolled from "Times Square," next to the mess hall, along "Broadway," the aisle beside the central three-tiered cellblocks, and having seen so little, felt that I had seen more than enough. I was glad to get back to the dock, to board the ferry that was returning, practically empty, to the mainland.

I took a cab south, for a trip about twice as far as I had walked, to the intersection of Bartlett and 23rd Streets. Thinking that the cabbie might be glad of the further information, I said, "It's in the Mission District," and was told rather snappily that, to be more exact, it was on the edge of the area called the Barrio, the Spanish term for a neighborhood. He added: "The way this city is going, guys like me, we're expected to know every frigging foreign language. The other day—I tell no lie—a fare got ratty with me because I didn't comprehend enough Cambodian. Cam-frigging-bodian, would you believe?" He continued in that vein, scowling at my sympathetic-looking reflection in his mirror, till we arrived.

I was there, not on a fool's errand, but on an errand that I suppose people with no interest in old crimes would consider foolish. I knew that the Emmanuel Baptist Church was demolished many years ago, that a school now occupies the site; but still I hoped to get a sense of what the immediate area was like, how it felt to live there, near the end of the nineteenth century—specifically, at Easter in 1895.

That year Easter Sunday fell on April 14. On the Saturday morning some women gathered at the church to arrange flowers for the services recalling the Resurrection. One of the women entered the library beside the altar. Noticing that the lock on the door to a smaller room was torn from its keep, she pushed the door open. She saw a scene of carnage. A woman's body lay, face up, on a table. The body had been stabbed many times, lastly in the chest, from which a broken dinner knife protruded; bits of the handle of the knife were scattered about, shining light brown amid dried splashes and puddles of blood. (None of the reports I have seen notes the presence or the unexpected absence of bloody footprints either within or leading from the room.) Clearly the woman who found the body was made of stern stuff: after summoning the other flower arrangers, she left them in their various states of distress and hastened to inform the pastor, George Gibson, who lived in a nearby boarding house.

It may be that the Reverend Gibson's odd reaction to the events arose from the fact that too many of his predecessors had given the Emmanuel Baptist Church a bad name: one of the first pastors had committed the sin of suicide by cutting his throat in his study in the church; another, Isaac Kallogh, had shot to death a newspaper proprietor with whom he had fallen out over politics (tried for murder, he was acquitted); and Gibson had come to the church, only five months before, to replace a minister who had been fired because he was "carrying on so with the womenfolk."

Gibson, who was a native of the Scottish capital, Edinburgh, had migrated to America in 1888, when he was twenty-nine. His sandy hair and large gray eyes gave an impression of weakness, which was contradicted by his athletic build. His conduct of services was not altogether conventional in that he would sometimes break off from reading a lesson or delivering a sermon to sing an aria from grand opera, not even bothering to translate the words into English.

On the Saturday morning, when told of the discovery at the church, he did not go there immediately but waited till he could be accompanied by one of the church's trustees. He stayed there only a minute or

The Reverend George Gibson.

two before dashing off—to an undertaker, who refused to do as he asked, which was to remove the body at once so as to "avoid publicity." By the time he got back to the church, the trustee had called the police.

Soon afterward the janitor turned up. He said that he had been at the church early that morning, before the arrival of the flower arrangers, and, noticing the damage to the door in the library, had reported the matter to the Reverend Gibson, who was working in his study. The pastor had said that he had already noticed the damage: "I'll have it investigated," he had said. "Meanwhile say nothing about it." Gibson agreed that the janitor's account was correct. In order to believe that both men told the truth, one has to believe that both of them were extraordinarily apathetic—that though each of them had noticed that a locked door had been forced open, neither had bothered to push it

Blanche Lamont and Minnie Williams.

farther open to see if there were indications within the small room as to *why* it had been broken into.

By midday, Gibson's hope of avoiding publicity was visibly hopeless. Word had spread like wildfire, and the intersection of Bartlett and 23rd Streets was crammed with chattering sightseers.

The general belief was that the murder victim was a twenty-one-year-old girl named Blanche Lamont, a member of the Emmanuel congregation and much involved in social activities of the church, who had been missing for ten days. She had last been seen—*definitely* seen—on the afternoon of Wednesday, April 3, when she had boarded a streetcar with a young man who had met her outside the Normal School, on the northern edge of the Mission District, where she was studying to be a teacher.

But the general belief was wrong. Once the blood was washed from the face, the body was recognized as that of a nineteen-year-old maidservant, Marian "Minnie" Williams, who had lived in the Mission District—and been a member of the Emmanuel congregation—till she had gained employment at Alameda, a town on the eastern edge of San

Francisco Bay. On Good Friday, having been given a few days off, she had come to stay with friends in the district and had left them at eight in the evening, meaning to attend a meeting of the Christian Endeavor Society at the home of an Emmanuel deacon on Bartlett Street. She had not been seen again—or rather, had not *definitely* been seen.

Going by one account of the case (each of the accounts I have read contains details that are absent from the others), a library card belonging to Blanche Lamont was found on the floor of the small room. If that is true, then the fact—no doubt about it—that nearly twenty-four hours passed before the police got round to searching the entire building means that they were not only slow but also slow witted. On the morning of Easter Sunday, the services cancelled, a detective climbed the circular steps to the belfry—actually to a platform near the top of the spire: there was no bell.

There he found the body of Blanche Lamont. She had been strangled. The body lay neatly supine, feet together, arms akimbo, the head resting on a wooden block. It was nude. The clothes, some of them torn, were tucked between floorboards and rafters: shoes, stockings, gloves, a large felt hat with plumes, bodice, skirt, corset, a corset cover, a corset waist, a sateen combination petticoat and waistband, under-flannels, and a pair of black "equestrienne tights."

Till the discovery of the second body, the sole suspect as the murderer of Minnie Williams was the Reverend Gibson, who had acted so oddly just before and shortly after the discovery of *her* body. Now, however, a twenty-four-year-old Canadian-born medical student, Theodore Durrant, became the sole suspect as the murderer of both girls.

Excepting hearsay, nothing in his background seemed to support the suspicion. A teetotaler and nonsmoker, he found time from his studies to serve as a bugler in the California National Guard—and to be a leading light of Emmanuel Church, acting as librarian, secretary of the Christian Endeavor Society, and assistant superintendent of the Sunday school. Police suspicion of him appears to have been based on two fragile grounds: one being that he bore a likeness to the man who had boarded a streetcar with Blanche Lamont on the day of her disappearance, the other being that he had subsequently visited her home and offered to help find her. (The police felt that the offer was suspi-

Theodore Durrant.

ciously overhelpful considering that, so far as anyone knew, Durrant
was no more friendly with Blanche than were other young men of the
Christian Endeavor Society.)

Durrant was arrested on the afternoon of Easter Sunday, after a message had been flashed on the new-fangled heliograph from Telegraph
Hill to a hill north of San Francisco, near where he was on duty with
the National Guard. A search of his home produced what appears to
have been the strongest evidence against him, an empty purse identified as Minnie Williams's. He claimed that he had found it while walking home along Bartlett Street after the meeting of the Christian Endeavor Society on the evening of Good Friday.

That evidence was inadmissible at his trial, which started on September 3, for he was charged only with the murder of Blanche Lamont.

The prosecution case was dependent on eyewitness evidence, much of which was tenuous (for instance, some people claimed to have seen Durrant with a young woman who *may* have been Blanche on the afternoon of April 3; others claimed to have seen Blanche with a young man who *may* have been Durrant that afternoon)—and some of the eyewitness evidence was devalued by the fact that the witnesses had been brought in to identify Durrant only after they had seen pictures of him in the papers.

The least credible of the eyewitnesses was a pawnbroker who happened to be known to the police as a buyer of stolen property. He was called in the hope that he would link Durrant with a most peculiar incident in the case. The day after Blanche's body was found, her aunt, with whom she had lived, had received a posted package containing three cheap rings belonging to her niece; the names of two prominent members of the Emmanuel Church were written in capital letters on the wrapping. The pawnbroker, ill at ease from the moment he took the stand and made more so by defense counsel's sarcastic questions, muttered that a man who may have been Durrant may have offered him a ring that may have been one of Blanche's on a day that may have been during the week after her disappearance.

The trial ran (using that word in the show-business sense) for just over eight weeks, which was a long time for a trial in 1895. I haven't done any sums, but I think that if the judge had not taken every opportunity for day-long adjournments (among the opportunities, holy days observed by Jews or Catholics, though he doesn't seem to have been either; a mysterious once-a-fortnight legal ritual known as Steamer Day; and his personal incommodities from head colds and an ingrown toenail), the proceedings would have lasted no more than a month. I suppose, though, that nowadays a similar trial would dawdle along for many months in America, almost as long in England—profitably for the lawyers but depressingly to anyone who still believes in the concept of justice, because it can be stated, as a general rule, that the unnecessary elongation of jury trials has reduced the likelihood of sensible verdicts, for several reasons: one being that juries grown bored and buttock sore will be inattentive; another being that, even if the jurors stay wide awake, they will not be able to see the wood for forests of artificial trees planted by counsel on both sides; and another being that some of the jurors will have been substandard from the start because many of the people called for jury service who have decent jobs and reasonable IQs, frightened at the prospect of virtual imprisonment for perhaps months on end, will have put forward accepted excuses (even lame ones will do in England) why their names should be crossed off the list, which means that the pools of prospective jurors are, in certain important respects, not up to scratch.

The trial of Theodore Durrant ended on November 1, when the jury retired, immediately agreed on the verdict, waited twenty minutes so as to give the impression that there had been some discussion, then returned with the verdict, which was that the defendant was guilty of murder in the first degree.

His lawyers lodged every possible appeal, even taking the case to the U.S. Supreme Court. Nearly two years after the trial, the last appeal was turned down. Durrant, still protesting his innocence, was hanged in San Quentin Prison on Friday, January 7, 1898. All of those who saw him die were impressed by his composure. One of them, a reporter for the *San Francisco Chronicle,* wrote: "Such fearlessness was made for better things than murder and its expiation. It may have come from vanity . . . but it was admirable."

The coffin was carried to a room near the execution chamber, where Durrant's parents were waiting. Food was brought to them. Rather than taking their appetites away, the emotional exhaustion had made them peckish. After a few ruminative minutes Mrs. Durrant, speaking with her mouth full, said, "Papa, I'll have some more of that roast."

Supposing that the unhappy cabbie had not been moaning away to himself while I was wandering around, he began again—frigging this, frigging that—the minute I returned. And so, to curtail the agony, I made a lame excuse for changing my return destination from Union Square, which is where the St. Francis is, to the stretch of Market Street bordering the Civic Center. Although he had done all of the talking— all on his favorite, I suspected only, subject—he said, "Nice talking with you," when I got out. Perhaps that was an automatic remark, said without thought to everyone he had tortured, even to passengers who had told him to shut up at the start. It made a change from "Have a nice day," which has been crooned at me, setting my teeth on edge, near midnight.

The Civic Center spreads over so many acres and consists of so many buildings (most of them white, some for government of one sort or another, others places of entertainment) that it is hard to make out where the center of it is. City Hall has a vast dome—vaster, I reckoned, than that on St. Paul's Cathedral. I supposed that it was the same City Hall as the one prefixed "New" in 1895, which was where the Durrant trial was held.

As I strolled along Market Street, I saw a woman who looked old pushing a wheeled hospital stretcher; blankets and clothes were piled high on the stretcher, and there were four diverse dogs on it, one at each corner, all sitting bolt upright as if they had been taught to. I hoped that my own dog, a spoilt cocker spaniel named Corny, was behaving himself while I was away; like one of P. G. Wodehouse's many dogs, Corny (who is named after Cornelius Howard, the first of the separately acquitted defendants in the superbly ornate Gorse Hall murder case, which I have written about) "never growls except as comedy."

Farther along Market Street, I saw a man pushing an apparently one-legged woman in a supermarket trolley that had been made into a sort of pram by the removal of the front struts; she was holding a cardboard sign, "CANNOT LIVE WITHOUT YOUR HELP," in one hand, a collection tin in the other. When they reached the corner, she, quite openly, got out of the trolley, massaged the leg she had been sitting on, and emptied the contents of the tin into a large bag, already bulging with notes and coins, that hung from her shoulders; the man took her place on the trolley, one of *his* legs doubled out of sight, and, as soon as he had the sign and the tin, was wheeled by the woman.

The slight scene prompted me to remember the little apparently one-armed Hispanic chap who had tried to steal from me the day before I set off on this trip; and as a postscript to the recollection, I hoped he had needed hospital treatment on his thieving arm. Pickpockets and speculative panhandlers—I see no immoral difference between them; no criminal difference either, whatever the statutes say. Begging has become a trade—a lucrative, tax-free trade, the proceeds of which are no doubt augmented by social-security handouts. This applies to

The St. Francis Hotel, San Francisco.

London too, where, for instance, young women sit by the steps to Underground railway stations, pleading for money to buy food for the babies in their arms who have been hired from their real mothers.

I found my way back to the St. Francis, went up to my room (only to hide the embarrassing Alcatraz carrier bag), and then went up to the twelfth floor, which seemed to be the top floor of this original part of the hotel, facing Union Square. The walls of the long corridor were covered with framed photographs of famous people who had occupied suites, not just rooms, on that floor. I didn't see a photograph of Roscoe "Fatty" Arbuckle. Come to think of it, I suppose he is no longer famous.

By the late summer of 1921, Arbuckle, who had risen from the ranks of the Keystone Kops, making his name in a long series of "Fatty and

Roscoe "Fatty" Arbuckle.

Mabel" movies with Mabel Normand, was second only to Charlie Chaplin as a cinema box-office attraction. As a result of an incident at the St. Francis on Labor Day, he became, by the end of the following week, a has-been.

With two friends, an actor and a director, he drove from Hollywood to San Francisco, arriving in the late afternoon of Saturday, September 3, and booking into a reserved suite at the St. Francis. (The L-shaped suite of three rooms—a bedroom on each side of a parlor, number 1220— is at the foot of a short corridor off the main one.)

The following day, three other people came to San Francisco from Hollywood. They booked into a hotel that did not live up to its name, the Palace. One of the trio was an actors' agent. Another was a friend of his, Maude "Bambina" Delmont. Presently describing herself as a gown model, she had a long police record for a diversity of fairly minor crimes, including "badger game" blackmail of married men with whom she had slept. The third member of the trio was a twenty-five-year-old aspiring movie actress, Virginia Rappe (she was careful to pronounce her name "Rap-pay"), whose one claim to fame was that her photograph had appeared on the sheet music of the song "Let Me Call You Sweetheart." She had a lot of very dark hair, noticeably large teeth, was five feet seven inches tall, and weighed nearly 140 pounds. According to Arbuckle's friend Buster Keaton, "She was about as virtuous as most of the other untalented young women who had been knocking around Hollywood for years, picking up small parts any way she could."

In the early afternoon of Monday, September 5—Labor Day—the small-time agent, the so-called gown model, and the unsuccessful actress were among a crowd of guests and gatecrashers at a party thrown by Arbuckle in the parlor of his suite. There was an abundance of top-quality bootleg booze, but Virginia Rappe, so it is said, was abstemious compared with most of the partygoers and showed no signs of inebriation when, at some time after two o'clock, she followed Arbuckle into his bedroom.

About half an hour later she was heard screaming. Arbuckle opened the bedroom door. Maude Delmont was the first of a number of people who went into the room. Virginia Rappe was lying on the bed, tearing at her clothes. She was still screaming, now explicitly, to the effect that she was suffering from terrible pains in her lower abdomen. She was carried to the bathroom, where some women undressed her and put her in a bath of cold water. A doctor who was called made a perfunctory examination and concluded that the pains were an effect of drinking on an empty stomach. She was taken to a vacant room. Other doctors who saw her took a time-is-the-greater-healer attitude to her pains. But as she was still suffering on Thursday, she was removed to a sanatorium. She died there the next day. A postmortem examination showed that her bladder was ruptured; death was ascribed to peritonitis. That examination was carried out illegally since permission for it had not been obtained from a coroner.

Those details are the only certain ones that emerge from a hotchpotch of often-contradictory statements.

So far as is known, Maude Delmont did not, either directly or indirectly, get in touch with Arbuckle or a boss of his studio, Paramount, before making allegations against him. The nub of her statement was that she, the first to enter the bedroom, had heard Virginia Rappe say: "I am hurt. I am dying. *He did it,* Maudie." On the basis of the allegations, Arbuckle was charged under the section of the penal code that provided that "a life taken in rape or attempted rape is considered murder."

There were immediate extralegal repercussions. Managers of cinemas that had been doing standing-room-only business with Fatty Arbuckle "romps," advertised as "Fun for All the Family," changed programs in midweek; distributors cancelled contracts for movies of his that were awaiting release.

The legal proceedings should have resulted in legal proceedings against lawyers on both sides. Maude Delmont, the instigator of the charge against Arbuckle, was not called as a witness, the reason being that Matthew Brady, the district attorney of San Francisco, feared that the defense, knowing of a particular shady aspect of her shady past, would use the information to discredit her—and in doing so would ruin the prosecution's entire case. Trying to make up for the absence of the star witness, Brady persuaded secondary witnesses to "improve" their evidence and arranged for others who might help the defense to be hidden away. Tit for tat, the defense also resorted to illegal tactics.

Unsurprisingly, considering the gaps in the evidence on both sides and the obvious lies told by several witnesses, the jury was unable to reach a verdict. A second trial also resulted in a hung jury (as at the first, there was a majority of 10–2 in Arbuckle's favor). At the third trial the jury took only five minutes to decide on acquittal. When the verdict had been announced, the foreman read out a statement that sounded suspiciously like a press agent's blurb: "Acquittal is not enough for Roscoe Arbuckle. We feel that a great injustice has been done him. . . . The happening at the hotel was an unfortunate affair for which Arbuckle, so the evidence shows, was in no way responsible. We wish him success."

That wish was not realized. The long-drawn-out, much publicized legal proceedings had made Fatty Arbuckle seem very unfunny. To make matters worse for him, Hollywood moguls reacted to the affair by appointing William Hays, a Presbyterian politician, as watchdog over the morality of movies and those who made them—in effect saying that, whether or not Arbuckle was a rapist and killer, he was guilty of bringing the whole industry into disrepute. Over the next decade he was occasionally employed in nightclubs and on the vaudeville stage, and, using the alias of William Goodrich (amended by wags to Will B. Good), he directed a few minor movies.

In 1933 it seemed that the has-been was making a comeback. Warner Brothers employed him in a series of two-reelers, then signed him up to appear in a full-length production. But the night the contract was agreed, Arbuckle died of a heart attack. He was forty-six. Some obituaries referred to "the lost years" with sadness, even a touch of shame. One paper, however, commented: "We no longer speak of him. . . . His death had been announced shortly after the disastrous party at the St. Francis Hotel, San Francisco."

(As virtually all show-business stars who visit San Francisco stay on the twelfth floor of the St. Francis, I suppose it would go against the law of averages if none of them died there. Even so, I think there must be some kind of coincidence in the fact that suite 1220, the scene of Fatty Arbuckle's "disastrous party" in September 1921, was where the singer Al Jolson died of a heart attack in October 1950. He had recently returned from an arduous tour of troop camps in Korea and was in San Francisco to make a guest appearance on a Bing Crosby wireless show from the Marines Memorial Club. I guess that Jolson is better known from impersonations of him, some as bad as that Amtrak conductor's, than from his recorded performances. I must admit that not long after his death, while I was a conscript in the Royal Air Force, my party piece was a futile attempt to sing "April Showers" as he did.)

There is another criminal case associated with the St. Francis.

Although Sara Jane Moore, a buxom, graying woman of forty-five, was sentenced to life imprisonment for attempting to assassinate the stand-in President Gerald Ford in 1975, it seems that she would have been most upset if the bullet she fired had injured him, let alone caused his death.

In 1973, soon after the annulment of her fifth marriage on the grounds that she had not bothered to divorce her fourth husband, she became acquainted with members of a few of the radical subversive groups that infested San Francisco at that time. While she was still trying to make sense of various quasi-Marxist philosophies, FBI agents asked for her help, and she, flattered, agreed to act as an informant.

After a couple of months, during which she became increasingly confused as to where her loyalties lay, she confessed to the radicals that
she was working for the FBI and was ostracized; the FBI warned her
that her life might be in danger. Desperately lonely, she sought the
forgiveness of the people she had been told to fear—but meanwhile
requested help from the FBI, who advised her to ask the police for
protection. After a few more months, she convinced the radicals that
she had repented and was ordered to act as an informant *against* the
FBI. Reinstated by the bureau, she became an entirely useless double
agent, passing tidbits of misinformation from one side to the other. By
the late summer of 1975, she was terrified that the radicals would suspect that information she had passed to the FBI had led to arrests: she
felt that she had to invent some dramatic means of proving her undivided loyalty to the Left.

I am not getting away from the story in saying that, on September 5,
Lynette "Squeakie" Fromme, an especially stupid disciple of the evil
megalomaniac Charles Manson, produced a gun in the vicinity of President Ford as he was walking across the capitol grounds in Sacramento
and was disarmed by a Secret Service agent. (Like Manson and those
disciples of his who, three years before, had been found guilty of mass
murder, she was sentenced to life imprisonment.)

Sara Jane Moore decided—or thought she decided—to emulate Lynette Fromme. Knowing that the president was to address a meeting of
the World Affairs Council at the St. Francis on Monday, September 22,
she bought a revolver. During the weekend—apparently having second thoughts, the idea now being that getting herself arrested as a
threat to the president was dramatic enough for her purpose—she
phoned the police and said that she planned to "test" the presidential
security system. The police called on her, confiscated the gun, and
informed the Secret Service, who interviewed her and concluded that
she was "not of sufficient protective importance to warrant surveil-
lance during the President's visit."

On the Monday morning she bought another gun and went to the
St. Francis, where she joined the crowd waiting at a side entrance on
Post Street to see the president when he left. Three hours passed. She
afterward explained: "There was a point when anything could have
stopped me and almost did. The most trivial little thing and I would

have said, 'Oh, this is ludicrous. What am I doing standing here?' . . .
I did try to leave once, but the crowd was just so tight. There was a
point where I thought, 'This has to be the most ridiculous thing I have
done in my entire life. What the hell am I doing here, getting ready to
shoot the President?' I turned around to leave. Couldn't get through
the crowd."

When the president emerged at half past three, she took the gun
from her purse and fired it at the wall of the hotel, from which the
bullet ricocheted against the heavy-trousered thigh of an off-duty cab
driver, causing a graze. Men standing near her pushed her to the ground,
and a policeman grabbed the gun. Some time after the president was
hastily driven away, she was taken into the hotel and there interviewed
in a reception room grotesquely named after Lucrezia Borgia. She was
perfectly happy—indeed, almost euphoric with relief—that now none
of her radical acquaintances could suspect that she was not wholly committed to the Fight to End Capitalist Domination or whatever catchphrase happened to be in fashion that day.

After lunch I made a sentimental journey—across the Bay Bridge to
the university town of Berkeley, which in England would be pronounced "Barkley." Toward the end of the 1960s, while I was complet-
ing my book on the killing of Julia Wallace, I knew that a book on the
case by an American author was being offered to English publishers—
and the knowledge frightened me, sometimes keeping me awake at
night, because I was convinced that if the American's book was accepted, no one would be interested in publishing another account:
mine. But the other book didn't appear. Soon after mine was published, I received a letter from the American author, Robert Hussey. I
am sure that if I had been in his shoes, either I wouldn't have written
or I would have written a brief note of insincere congratulation. His
letter, several pages long, read like a rave review.

I replied at once—and that was the start of a correspondence between us, frequent and regular, that lasted till his death. I met him
when he and his wife, K, short for Katherine, came to England; I was
able to find a publisher for his book. After Bob's death, I kept up a
correspondence with K. That, in turn, lasted till she died a few years
ago. They were dear friends. And so this afternoon I went to where

they had lived, which I had known, from snapshots, was a bungalow with a large garden sloping down from it. A bit misty eyed, I am glad to admit, I visualized Bob sitting in the garden, tapping a letter to me on his portable Remington, while K (who always handwrote her letters) pottered among her flowers, some of which—most, I hoped—were still helping toward the blaze of colors. The new owners were not at home, nor was the only neighbor whose name I know. But still, I am glad that I went. At least I have seen the place where hundreds of letters were written to me, where hundreds of mine were read. Now it is more than just a postal address that I shall always know by heart: 936 Creston Road, Berkeley, California 94708, U.S.A.

Back at the St. Francis, I changed into my Sunday-best suit and, on the way out again, cashed a travelers' check, asking for quarters as well as notes as I wanted to test the efficiency of "the world's only legal money launderer." In 1938, when the silver dollar was the coin of the realm, the hotel's manager ordered that any to be given as change were to be cleaned so as to save women guests' white gloves from being grubbied; a cutlery-polishing machine was adapted, and a man employed full-time to operate it. The money-laundering operation, continuing, has become a tradition. According to a press release, San Franciscans refer to clean silvery coins as "St. Francis money"; in 1991 the mayor named a day after the current cleaner, who, then close to ninety, had been doing the job for thirty years, during which time he had dealt with about $17 million, weighing more than a million pounds. There.

I had spruced myself up to have dinner with George Raine and his wife, Kay, who is, and looks as if she is, a dancer, at the Washington Square Grill, which George had told me was the favorite eating and drinking place for "the city's writing crowd." Stupid of me, but I had not thought that there were Washington Squares other than the one in Manhattan. That was the first place I visited on the first morning of my first trip to America. After an early breakfast at the Algonquin, I walked down Fifth Avenue—and was depressed to find that the square I *knew* from Edwardian tales had lost all of its elegance, was no lovelier than a pig pen, a garbage tip; even the splendid arch, designed by Stanford White, was scruffy, the lower parts daubed with painted messages and spattered, slightly less literately, with excrement.

San Francisco's Washington Square, close to Telegraph Hill, is much nicer: grassy and tree strewn, with tidy paths along which, when I was there, people released from work were pleased to saunter, and young women, some appearing to be nursemaids, guided prams or walked sedately alongside haphazard children. Arriving early, I sat on a bench and wished I had arrived earlier, to sit longer, enjoying the quiet ordinariness.

The eponymous grill was crowded, especially near the bar, where the Raines were waiting for me, already wondering, for they knew of my knack of getting lost, whether one of them should go looking for me. It was good to see them again. Doing as I had been asked by a friend at home, a founder-member of CAMRA, the Campaign for Real Ale, I tried one of the "steam beers" made in small local breweries and, finding that it actually tasted like beer, unlike the mass-marketed lager-stuff, all fizz and no flavor, had another. George's description of the place when we had spoken on the phone had left me wondering whether it would be crammed with journalists, as El Vino's was till London newspapers deserted Fleet Street; or with "creative" employees of advertising agencies, like Groucho's now; or with women, certain men too, wearing peasant costumes and speaking iambically, which is too often so at the Arts Club. But, I must say to my relief, the customers of the grill seemed as motley as regulars in an English pub.

The dinner was very good. As I hadn't seen the Raines for some years (the last time was in London), we had a lot to catch up on: too much, and so we continued the evening, the night, at an otherwise customerless Amelio's, close by on Powell Street, perched on high stools at the counter—and, referring to myself, feeling like a detail of an Edward Hopper painting. I do believe that talking with old friends is the one surely abiding pleasure in life.

To Benson

A nother early start: a bus at 8:10, arriving at Oakland Station a quarter of an hour before the train left for Los Angeles, having come all the way south, well over a thousand miles, from Vancouver; the whole route is called the Coast Starlight. From Oakland, the tracks follow *El Camino Real*—the royal road—along which Franciscan monks built twenty-five missions, or chapels, each a day's journey on horseback from the next.

I was going to Los Angeles only to catch another train, starting me on the return part of my trip. Especially as the delay in getting to San Francisco had cost me one of the two evenings I should have spent there, I would have liked a second full day in the city. But that had never been possible, for trains run only three times a week on the Sunset Limited, the route east from Los Angeles.

The fact that the eleven-hour journey to Los Angeles was in aid of catching another train may have put me in the wrong frame of mind for window gazing. Perhaps I missed some uncluttered views of the Pacific. Whenever I saw it, there was a messy hem of ticky-tacky bungalows and mobile homes (which surely ought to be called once-mobile homes, for they are towed to places where, wheel-less, they are either repainted in eyesore colors or left to rot). I was reminded, against my will, of the miles of the northern coast of Wales that have been polluted by caravan parks. I find it mystifying that the settlers there, like those here, have blithely befouled the beauty that must have attracted them to the area.

The train reached San Luis Obispo, one of the mission towns, in the early afternoon. I noticed it only because the Amtrak route guide mentioned that San Simeon isn't far away. If I ever come back to California, I shall try to get there, just to see whether William Randolph Hearst's castle, La Casa Grande, is anything like *Citizen Kane*'s Xanadu.

There was an odd couple on the train. One of the men was very large, the other very small, and they both wore Egyptian-style, upside-down-flowerpot hats covered with green baize, yet were countenanced as mournfully as morticians. Regular as clockwork, every three-quarters of an hour or so they marched past where I was sitting alone, pretending that the seat next to me was taken, and a few minutes later marched back. The large man always led the way, with the teeny-weeny one following like a visual echo. I silently christened them Bill and Ben the Flowerpot Men. I asked the elderly woman across the aisle if their hats signified that they were members of a fraternal order like the Oddfellows, and she said she thought they were "more likely your everyday pair of loonies." I told her the story about Noel Coward watching the procession of open carriages taking foreign dignitaries to the coronation of Elizabeth II. One of the carriages contained the extraordinarily vast Queen Salote of the South Pacific island of Tonga and, cramped beside her, a tiny Oriental. Coward was asked who the little man was. "That," he explained in his clipped way, "is the Queen's elevenses." The story must have lost something in my telling of it, for the elderly woman only nodded gravely.

The train arrived at Los Angeles a few minutes early. But according to every clock on the station, and there were lots of them, it had arrived an hour late. Worried that the clocks were correct, which is surely to be expected of railway-station clocks, and that I had neglected to alter my watch between time zones, I fretted at the thought that I would go to catch my next train in three hours' time and find that it had left an hour ago—which would leave me stuck in Los Angeles for two days.

I went to the ticket counter and asked the one assistant on duty there to tell me the time. "I'm paid just to sell tickets, man," he growled. "You want information—you go to the guy at Information who's paid to give information." While wondering if he was related, perhaps illegitimately, to the unhelpful painter of the Lexington Hotel in Chicago, I pointed out that the part of the counter marked Information was deserted. "You suggesting the information guy ain't entitled to a break?" the "assistant" enquired. As he had inadvertently left his own watch visible, allowing me to see that the time on it was the same as on mine, I changed the subject, asking where I could leave my luggage. "At check-in," he grunted—and added with radiant delight: "But the check-in guy's taking his break. Hang around, and you may catch him opening up. No guarantee, mind." I decided that if I did manage to catch the elusive check-in guy, it would create the worry that he would be taking another break throughout the hour or so before my train left.

I had intended to kill some of the between-trains time by taking a trip around Los Angeles, but, lumbered with luggage, I couldn't. That was probably just as well, for there was nothing in midtown that I specially wanted to visit, and I was determined not to look at Hollywood, as I wanted to preserve my mind-picture of the glamorous place that it seems to have been.

The station waiting area was easily the grandest I had ever seen. Actually, one cannot see much of it at night because the illumination from the enormous square chandeliers is inadequate, making no more than a brownish mist at floor level, certainly nothing like enough to read by. But from what I could make out, the building looks like a seventeenth-century Spanish palace that a twentieth-century designer had tried to modernize with touches of art deco. All but one thing in it is brown: the massively beamed ceiling, the walls, the marble floor, and the rows of high-backed, thronelike leather armchairs, only some of which have been slashed by vandals. One gets an optical illusion that the brownness has seeped through the tall windows into the brown-lit courtyards on each side; the brown-leaved palm trees there look as if they are deciduous, tinctured by an everlasting autumn.

A corner of the waiting area is lit as harshly white as an operating theater. That is a café called McCarthy's—which is a strange name for a café entirely staffed by Hispanics and where Hispanic food is about all one can buy. When I was there, the menu consisted of only two dishes: a congealed mess that I surmised had once upon a time resembled chili, and things called (if I heard aright) burrinos, which were sausage-shaped lumps of gray mincemeat. I bought half a dozen packets of salted crackers and a mug of cola, and, finding that the crackers were long past their sell-by date, as floppy as dough, and that the mug smelt of condemned dishrags, left them on one of the mucky tables.

Every so often a voice snarled through the loudspeakers that anyone caught smoking would be ejected from the station, but as I saw a number of people, including Amtrak employees, puffing away, I carried my luggage to a particularly murky corner and followed suit. After three unblissful hours, a different voice sighed in a "So what's new?" tone that, owing to an oversight, there had been no announcement that the train of the Sunset Limited was ready for boarding, and if passengers didn't get a move on, they would miss it. Convinced that the announcement hadn't been given because the announcer had sloped off for a break, I joined the rush.

Even before the train left, I had fixed the bed in my roomette and fallen into it. I went straight to sleep and didn't wake up till eight o'clock, when the attendant, a friendly little white chap named Eamon, brought coffee. He said that we were running late but were about two hundred miles into Arizona; that we had passed Phoenix and were heading toward Tucson via Coolidge.

In the restaurant car I sat opposite two men who looked old. Their faces were as brown and crinkled as walnuts. Both wore wide-brimmed hats, tartan shirts with kerchiefs, and leather waistcoats that appeared to be homemade. They were finishing breakfast when I arrived but told the waiter "same again" when I ordered mine; they finished their second breakfasts while I was still eating. They told me that they were prospectors. One introduced himself as Barney; the other invited me to call him Bud, explaining, "My name ain't really Bud, but my family name is Wise, which ain't altogether accurate in my case, so I'm known as Bud Wise, like the beer—you understand my meaning?"

I said that I did. I asked them what they prospected for, and Barney said: "Anything we happen on. We don't, as the saying is, specialize. Silver . . . gold—even fool's gold and them itty-bitty pretty pebbles: we sell that junk to imitation-jewelry guys—bijouterologists is what they call themselves, would you believe?"

I asked if they had ever struck lucky. Barney said, "Oh, sure," and Bud said: "Frequent as fleas. But being lucky ain't nowhere near as crucial as feeling lucky—right, Barney?" He pointed through the window toward distant hills. "When you're out there, hoping to find what you ain't necessarily looking for, and not giving a damn if you don't: that's what feeling lucky is all about"—which made me think enviously of David Mittell's unoptimistic pleasure from fishing.

Bud asked me where I was heading.

"Benson," I said.

Their faces became crinklier. Barney said: "If you're not offended by the enquiry, why in tarnation are you going to that half-a-horse town? Never heard of nobody going to Benson 'cepting by accident."

I explained that I had been assured that I could catch a bus from there to Tombstone.

"A bus?" they said, speaking in unison and then peering at each other and shaking their heads. Barney said: "Well, sir, I hope—but I ain't confident—you've been told right. Can't remember the last time I saw any bus 'cepting a long-haul Greyhound in that territory. You, Bud?"

"Me neither."

Barney got up, and so did Bud, and they both banged their heels on the floor, rather like clog dancers in Lancashire, presumably to loosen their boots, and then tapped the brims of their hats and said "feel lucky" instead of "goodbye."

I concluded that I had no choice: I *had* to feel lucky. If I didn't get off at Benson, my subsequent Amtrak bookings and hotel reservations would be out of kilter.

I needed to wait a few minutes before leaving the restaurant car as the exit was blocked by a young man just arriving for breakfast. I hoped he hadn't had to come far. He had a black eye, and one of his arms was in plaster, as was one of his legs. When he at last managed to squeeze halfway onto a seat, he pantingly apologized for the holdup, revealing that some of his teeth were missing. As I passed him, trying not to stare, I saw that the back of his t-shirt said "STUNTS UNLIMITED. We Never Fall Down on a Job."

The horizons are always hilly, and the hills prod the clouds above them into crazy patterns. I saw, miles from anywhere, what looked like a scene from a science-fiction movie: in the distance, enormous white globes surrounded by a wire fence (a nuclear establishment, I surmised), and, like an army from another planet, seeming to be marching toward the globes, hundreds of cactus plants as tall as tall trees, their bloated arms pushing almost to the sandy ground. I saw, for the first time, cotton fields: a lovely sight made lovelier by the barrenness all around—lint-white blobs on acres of dark green. I saw thousands of toy-balloon-sized red balls that I thought at first were floating in the air; it turned out they were threaded like beads onto electrical lines as a warning to crop-dusting airplanes. I saw some of those, flying so low that their shadows were almost as large as they were; and I recalled, of course, the murderous crop duster in *North by Northwest*—and wondered, as I have since the second time I saw that splendid partial re-hash of episodes from earlier Hitchcock movies, why on earth Roger O. Thornhill had to dash around the lonely bus stop like a volunteer victim instead of lying doggo in the acres of tall corn; panic is a perfectly good reason for odd behavior in real life, but I don't think it should be used as the only reason for particular thrills in fiction.

The train reached Benson at half past eleven. I was the only one who got off; nobody got on. I felt like Spencer Tracy at the start of *Bad Day at Black Rock*. He had only one arm, but I had a lot more luggage.

It was very hot: close to 110 degrees, I learned later. The train was soon on its way, bell jingling and siren whooping as if in celebration of early release from Benson, and I was still standing by the track. I did not feel lucky. There was no need to look far to the left or right to see the whole of Benson, cuddled against this side of the rails. I saw it through a fuzz of dust that the movement of the train had made and rather wished that the movement had made a fog, sufficiently pea-soupish, like the ones we used to have in London, to make the place invisible.

There were no surprising sights—no pedestrians, for instance. After asking the attendant at the filling station, a woman behind the counter in a knitting-wool shop (its trade surely single seasonal), and a man lolling in a truck (who was not well pleased to be asked as I had woken him up to do so), I was left in no doubt that Bud and Barney were

Benson, Arizona, from the train stop.

right: there was no bus to Tombstone—no bus to anywhere. Addition-
ally upsetting, I had been told that there was neither a cab nor a hire-
car service in Benson—and that as Tombstone, twenty-five miles to
the southeast, was not on the way to anywhere apart from somewhere
called Bisbee, which hardly any Bensonians ever needed to visit, I had
virtually no hope of cadging a lift.

Dragging my luggage, I entered the Horseshoe Saloon. The inevi-
table Muzak machine was playing a record of an Italian tenor screaming, as if he really meant it, an aria from *Turandot,* "None Shall Sleep."

A tiny barmaid trilled: "Hi, I'm Olga. How may I enhance your pleasure?"

I asked if Benson had a telephone, and she directed me down a corridor leading to the lavatories; she also handed me a leaflet that I gathered was the local telephone book. I rang the hotel in Tombstone, where
I was supposed to be spending the next two nights, and asked the
woman who answered how I could get there from Benson. "Only with
considerable difficulty," she said, chortling at the little joke as if it were
original. I asked if she could arrange for a car to collect me, she, still
chortling, said no, and I banged the phone down. I rang the Benson
Police Station, explained my predicament to the girl who eventually

answered, was told that I had one hell of a problem, asked if she could suggest a solution to it, was told no, hung up, and went back to the bar.

By then Olga had turned me into An Event. All of the customers, all of whom were wearing cowboy costumes, examined me, as did the kitchen staff, taking turns to peep round the edge of the swing door, and when I ordered a beer, Olga's colleague, a tall woman who introduced herself as Sharon, insisted on pouring it, meanwhile saying that I was the first Britisher to come to Benson since only the good Lord knew when.

While Sharon was at the till, getting my change, I, miserably re-signed to being stuck in Benson for two whole days, asked Olga if there was a hotel. "Well, no, not so you'd notice," she said, "but there's a motel kind of establishment a bit along the way"—whereupon Sharon let out a shriek and said: "Landsakes, Olga, you ain't got the brains you was born with, suggesting that this gentleman should stay THERE! You surely haven't forgotten what happened to the last poor soul you sent to that place."

While I was having visions of the Bates's Motel in *Psycho,* she brought me back into the conversation, saying: "You just gotta stay at the Quail Hollow. It's on the edge of town, but as you've no doubt gathered, the edge of this town is in spitting range of the middle." She knew the telephone number and told me to mention her name, thus making me suspicious that she got commission on business she touted.

I phoned the Quail Hollow, which turned out to be a motel. A woman said yes, there were vacancies, and sure, she could get Chuck the handy-man to collect me from the saloon in his wagon, then made my blood boil by asking how he would recognize me. Speaking louder than I had for a long time, I told her that it couldn't be simpler, as I was the only customer not dressed like Roy Rogers.

Chuck, who arrived only a few minutes later, was a muscular young man with blond hair bleached white by the sun. He lifted my case onto his wagon as if it were as light as a six-pack of cornflakes. On the way to the Quail Hollow, he told me that he was a native of Tucson; that he had recently "emigrated" to Benson with his wife and children "be-cause Tucson has become a dangerous place to live. I've heard tell it used to be known as a shit-kicking town—on account of all the horse traffic, y'see—but now it's the shit that does the kicking. Undesirable elements, if you catch my drift. I don't earn as much here, but the wife and me, we reckon that it's better for us and the kids to be safe and poor than rich and dead. We're pleased we moved here. We're real happy."

The Quail Hollow was new but not excessively modern. It was built around a courtyard that had a swimming pool. My room was very nice. There was no restaurant, but just across the road was a café called the Plaza, open twenty-four hours a day, where people staying at the motel could get 10 percent off their bills by showing their room key. I went there at once and had a large steak, cooked just as I had asked it to be, and more strawberry jello and whipped cream than I could cope with.

My inability to get to Tombstone proved to be a blessing in disguise. I spent two blissful, lazy days in Benson. The middle-of-the-day temperature was never below 100 degrees, but as there was no humidity, the heat was bearable, even pleasurable; any sweat I made was dried away the minute it appeared. Of my several memories of the place, two of natural things will certainly stay with me. The unkempt roadside near the Quail Hollow was scattered with thousands of tiny black chips, and as one got within an alarming footstep of any of them, they became butterflies, deep red and dark brown, fluttering every which way like confetti in a breeze. And there was the miracle of the double sunsets—the first, garish as candy floss, lasting a long while but not long enough, and after a few minutes on the edge of darkness, the bashful encore of greens and blues and half-hearted purples.

Perhaps other places in Arizona have similar surprising butterflies, similar double sunsets, but I doubt if any town in the state has such genial inhabitants. I must have seen each of the adults at least twice, and each of them, second time round, at least called out, "How y' doing?" "Pleased to see you," or "Have a nice day" as if they really meant it. Five of them, having heard why I was in Benson, offered to drive me to Tombstone.

Two of those who offered I had met first at the little historical society, where the pièce de resistance is a Victorian dentist's chair that may—only may, mind—have been used by Doc Holliday. The place, otherwise cluttered with old bean cans and bottles and funny-shaped stones, reminded me of the attempt at a local museum in one of E. F. Benson's "Lucia" novels—*Lucia in London,* I think. I was given the tour and was told that the town had its beginnings in 1860, with the establishment of a stopover depot on the Butterfield Stagecoach run between Dragoon Pass and Tucson, and that twenty years later it became a railhead on the Southern Pacific—"fast growing but not to decent people's taste. It had seven saloons and a bawdy house considered one of the most elaborate in the West, catering to riffraff such as gunfighters, remittance men, and fastbuck artists."

I turned down all five offers of a lift to Tombstone, for I had convinced myself that I wouldn't like the place and didn't want to be proved wrong. That was not a species of sour grapes. Before I got to Benson, thinking that I was going to Tombstone, I had had misgivings about going there. The publicity material I had been sent had given the strong impression that Tombstone was not so much a town as a Wild West theme park; one of the leaflets had referred to a waxwork tableau of the Gunfight at the OK Corral, and if the map in the same leaflet was accurate, then the pay-at-the-gate corral was not where the real one was. Now, perfectly contented in Benson, I decided that I didn't want to say more about the episode than the little bit I had already written:

Ike Clanton was the only member of the Clanton gang left alive after the gunfight at the OK Corral on Tuesday, October 25, 1881; his colleagues, Billy Clanton and Frank and Tom McLowery, had been shot to death by U.S. Marshal Virgil Earp, his brothers Wyatt and Morgan (created deputies by Virgil), and the consumptive dentist and gambler, John Henry "Doc" Holliday. There seems no doubt that the gunfight was the culmination of a long-standing feud, but there are conflicting accounts of what happened in the corral—one suggesting that the fight was hardly fair, considering that none of the Clanton gang was armed.

One of the offers of a lift to Tombstone came from an old timer (that was how he spoke of himself) named Wolfe O'Meara. He scoffed at the "goodie-goodie" way the Earps were portrayed in movies, saying: "How come, then, that the brothers were known as 'The Fighting Pimps'? In them days—and this is an established fact—you could tell the difference between the real gunfighters and the pimps by the artillery they carried: the gunfighters all toted silver revolvers, and the pimps had pretty pearl-handled ones. The Earp brothers' guns were pearl-handled, and what's more—another established fact—there was a brother named Jim who stayed away from the OK Corral, and his wife, her name was Bessie, was listed in the street directory as 'sporting woman,' which was the delicate way of describing a prostitute."

Changing the subject, he said he guessed that I, being English, had heard of Jack the Ripper. "Well," he said, "I can tell you, as an established fact, that Jack the Ripper died right here in Benson." He explained:

The day before Thanksgiving in November 1906, all trains into and out of Benson were halted by a railwaymen's strike. Hundreds of passengers disembarked, and many of them killed time in the Wildcat Saloon, handily situated across from the depot, and which was owned by a hard-nosed citizen named Jesse Fisher and run by a man who was known only as Jack the Ripper—"He never divulged what his real name was, and nobody ever enquired, seeing as how guys like him could get real fierce with anybody that expressed interest in their past lives.

"Anyhow, the Wildcat did great business because of the strike—liquor flowed, the roulette wheel went on turning, the one-armed pianist played simple melodies, and the hostesses did OK at a dime a feel or whatever the going rate was. And Jack worked nonstop, all through the night and into the afternoon of Thanksgiving, when the crowd thinned a bit and him and Jesse Fisher had time to count the house profits, amounting to $612, a real tidy sum in them days. Fisher, who don't seem to have been exactly philanthropic, sacked up $600 for himself and handed the rest to Jack as a bonus for his endeavors. Jack weren't none to grateful, as you can imagine, and for the rest of the day he muttered 'stingy bastard' whenever he touched shoulders with Fisher.

"In the evening, his slow burn came to a boil. He pulled the house .45 from under the bar and shot out the big hanging oil-lamp and started shooting at Fisher; but I guess because he couldn't see too well in the dark, he only damaged Fisher with a slug in the hip. Fisher, it appears, was great at dollar arithmetic but lousy at counting shots. As soon as Jack had run out of ammunition and was just making inoffensive clicking noises, Fisher pulled out his own gun—to protect the clientele, so he afterwards said—and returned the previous fire, making a hole the size of a silver dollar in Jack's bellybutton, which caused him to be deceased. I can't vouch for this, but it's said that Fisher used the Ripper's stingy bonus to pay for the funeral expenses and get the oil-lamp fixed."

Wolfe O'Meara pointed to a building a few doors from the Horse-shoe, which is now Benson's only saloon. "That's where the Wildcat used to be," he said. "Now it's the local office of the H&R Block Co., the income tax experts. Things sure have changed." He sighed and added, "I guess for the better if you don't hold with excitement."

If I had not decided to use the laundry room at the Quail Hollow, I would not have met Betsy Ambrosia, would not have heard the strange story about her younger brother Charlie.

I had never used a washing machine and was trying to understand the from-the-Japanese instructions above those in the laundry room when a very old and battered sleeping van drew up outside the door, practically blocking it, and a dumpy little woman in her fifties got out, dragging a bag of dirty washing that was almost as large as she was. "You having difficulty?" she asked rhetorically, having observed my bafflement. I said yes, and she said, "Men." She took over, putting my few things in with hers. I introduced myself, and she said: "I'm Betsy Ambrosia. God's truth." While she pottered between one machine and another, she said that she and Charlie, who was resting in their room, had stopped off on their way from Las Vegas to their home in Florida.

Following the Vietnam War, Charlie, a regular marine, had been sent for special training at a camp near Las Vegas. While he was there, all of his near relatives and close friends were visited and interviewed by FBI agents—the reason being, so the agents said, that he was being considered for guard duty at the White House. When the family next heard from him, he was undergoing guerilla training on the island of Okinawa; the next they heard, he was preparing to go on a mission. They heard nothing from him for over a month.

Then Betsy, his next-of-kin, received a phone call from someone who said that he was speaking from the Pentagon but refused to give his name. The caller said that Charlie was the sole survivor from a small party of marines that had been ambushed by the Viet Cong; there had been a delay in identifying him as his pockets were empty and his dog tag was missing; he was not physically wounded but was suffering from amnesia and had already been sent to a military hospital near Washington, D.C. The caller refused to say which hospital and rang off. Betsy spent a useless "small fortune" in trying to learn Charlie's whereabouts.

A month or so after the call, a cab arrived at the family home. Two men helped Charlie out and pushed him toward the door, then scuttled back to the cab, which was immediately driven away. Charlie could remember nothing from the time he was at the camp near Las Vegas— nothing about the ambush—nothing about the period in hospital.

He still remembered nothing of those months. He suffered from seizures. For more than a quarter of a century, Betsy had looked after him, finding it hard to make both ends meet because he had been granted only a small retirement pension; the authorities had insisted that he had never been in Vietnam—had insisted that his disability had arisen from "non-active service" causes.

But a few months ago the authorities had, without explanation, granted Charlie a full disability pension. A check for a lump sum, covering what Betsy called "the lost years," had arrived, and she had asked Charlie how he would like to use part of it. He had said that he wanted to go to Las Vegas. "Charlie's not interested in gambling," she told me. "I believe he wanted to go to Vegas just in the hope of finding that camp, the last place he remembered before the memory gap. We searched around, asked around, but we couldn't find it. Still and all, I think Charlie's enjoyed the trip. Hard to tell, because he don't do much smiling. Speaking selfishly, I've had a fine time."

I thanked her for doing my washing. And I passed on the advice I had been given by Bud and Barney: "Feel lucky."

I had by then recalled some advice I was given years ago by Ewen Montagu, who is now dead, still missed. Taller than I am, visibly Jewish, and rarely separate from an elderly briar pipe that seemed to wheeze even when he wasn't puffing at it, he enjoyed a long and wonderfully full and varied life. During the Second World War, he, a senior intelligence officer, devised the scam of drifting a corpse, dressed up and decked out as a Royal Marine carrying top-secret plans, onto the Spanish coast, thereby confusing the Nazis as to where Allied forces would invade along the northern shores of the Mediterranean; after the war he told parts of that story in a book, *The Man Who Never Was*, which

The author with the Honorable Ewen Montagu at the latter's London home, 1983.

became a bestseller and was turned into a movie that he hated, not only because "he" was played by "a retired American chorus boy, that fellow Clifton Webb." He once told me, while sprawled in the bedraggled armchair that he had had made, its seat long enough for his long legs, that all through his adult life he had experienced disasters that turned out to be blessings (one, his being turned down for active service, had led to his concoction of the scam that fooled the Nazis, saving thousands of British Commonwealth and American lives)—so many blessed disasters, he added, that he had come up with a maxim. Grinning on the pipeless side of his face, for he knew that I had just received what seemed very bad news, he advised me to treat his maxim as advice, then repeated it, saying, "Pray for calamities."

Thinking of my unintended stay in Benson, I decided that there was something—by no means everything—in what Ewen had advised.

After I had had my last meal at the Plaza Café, Rosie, the head waitress on the morning shift, handed me a picture-postcard that said at the top "Hope to see you again" and that all of the waitresses had signed.

That was nice. I took a roundabout route back to the Quail Hollow, simply so as to walk among the black chips that turned into butter-flies. Chuck drove me to the train stop.

To New Orleans

Continuing on the Sunset Limited route, the first stop after Benson, three hours away, is Lordsburg, which is in New Mexico. Farther along, east of a town called Deming, there is an extinct volcano, the rock-hard lava reaching almost to the railway track. To the north is a town called Truth or Consequences, and farther north is the battleground of the Lincoln County War of the 1870s between gunfighters employed by the owners of two vast ranches; William "Billy the Kid" Bonney, who switched from one side to the other, that of an Englishman, John Tunstall, wreaked deadly vengeance on the sheriff who arranged the murder of Tunstall and was himself killed by the replacement sheriff, Pat Garrett, who received the reward of five hundred dollars that had been offered by Lew Wallace, the governor of New Mexico (and author of *Ben-Hur*).

After the stop at Deming, the train travels close to the Mexican border, at one point within ten yards of it, and crosses the Rio Grande River into Texas soon after teatime. I have heard a rhyme that used to be recited by travelers through the Lone Star State: "Sun is riz, sun is set, / Here we are in Texas yet." There is certainly a lot of it: a distance of about eight hundred miles from west to east—farther than from Land's End to John o'Groats, the longest distance on the British mainland.

At dinner, I sat opposite a middle-aged married couple named Myrna and Ham, short for Hamilton. Myrna, who did all the talking, told me that they were returning from Las Vegas to their home in Bogalusa, Louisiana, which they had never before been away from for more than a day, and that the trip was a present from her rich brother, Myron. As she and Ham were strictly religious, they had not gone into a casino, but as they both loved classical music, "them Johann Strausses and such-like," they had visited the Liberace Museum. The high spot of the trip had been a wonderful gourmet meal: the greatest tuna sandwich she had ever tasted. What had been done to it to make it so good, she, a better-than-somewhat cook, had no idea. Tuna would never taste the same again, because That Sandwich had not tasted like tuna. Her Rhapsody on the Theme of a Las Vegan Tuna Sandwich, reprised throughout my meal, was so mouth-watering as to make all that I ate seem humdrum.

During the night, the train passed through Langtry, which was once called Vinegarone; Roy Bean, the local saloonkeeper who in the 1880s set himself up as a judge, "the Law West of the Pecos," was so remotely enamored of the actress Lillie Langtry, the "Jersey Lily" who for some time was a mistress of the Prince of Wales who eventually became King Edward VII, that, presumably without opposition, he renamed the town after her. (I don't know how many death sentences were passed by Bean, but it was certainly nowhere near the 160 handed out by Isaac Parker during the twenty-one years from 1875 when he was a judge in the Arkansas–Oklahoma Territory.)

About an hour before I was awoken by Franklin, the black attendant, the train had stopped at San Antonio, otherwise known as the Mission City because of the five Franciscan missions, one of them the Alamo, in and around it. The landscape, which the evening before had been of many shades of brown, occasionally enlivened by lofty yucca plants, their seedy heads and leafy waists making them look like dancers in tutus, was now of many shades of green—an indication, I was told, that we were nearing the humid Gulf Coast. There were tin signs on tall poles: "Sportsmen, Please Don't Shoot at the Telephone Lines." I wondered if all the sportsmen used sporting guns. I am appalled by the free and easy arms trade in so many of the United States.

We reached Houston in the middle of the morning; Beaumont, the last stop in Texas, at lunchtime. With due respect to Texas, I was not sorry to be coming to the end of it. We crossed the Sabine River into Louisiana. I stared at the cypress swamps, looking out for alligators, but, unless I mistook some as being fallen trees, did not see any. Once when I was in Manhattan, walking up Fifth Avenue, a woman wearing a trilby, sunglasses, and a black cape dashed out of the Sherry-Netherland Hotel and into a limousine, and a passerby frantically shouted at me: "*That was Garbo!*" The limousine was gone by the time he assured me of the truth of his italicized statement. That made one of the irritating sadnesses of my life—the fact that I shall never know whether or not I actually SAW GARBO. Since one tends to remember one's memories of small incidents rather than the incidents themselves, it probably won't be long before I am convinced that I saw her. (I believe that the remembering-memories phenomenon is an important reason why eyewitness evidence is so unreliable.)

And that reminds me that, on one of my nights in Benson, I switched on the television and watched, though not for long, a cops-and-robbers movie—switching it off dismissively when, as almost always happens in such shows, a cop (but it could be a lawyer or a cheeky crook) shook his head in a disdainful way and said something like, "Oh, sure, but the evidence against so-and-so is only circumstantial"—all but stating that circumstantial evidence is invariably second-rate. Which is utter nonsense. Someone should tell the writers of such tosh that there are only two sorts of legal evidence. There is the *direct* sort—from eye or ear witnesses—and the rest, every single bit of it, excepting formal evidence such as maps and plans, is *circumstantial.* Since most major crimes go unwitnessed, most detectives would be transferred to traffic duty, most courts and prisons would be closed, and almost everyone wanting to commit crime would go ahead unconcernedly if circumstantial evidence were as useless as those writers (and nearly all reporters of trials) make it out to be. I fear that, as so many jurors rely on television for their legal knowledge and believe so much of what they see and hear, it has become easier for shady defense lawyers to fool them into thinking that cast-iron evidence, because it is called "circumstantial," should be disregarded. It would be interesting, certainly of more interest than surveys of people's views on the Hidden Meanings of the Lesser-Known Plays of Samuel Beckett or Einstein's Special Theory of Relativity, if an honest pollster were to ask a sample of prospective jurors for *their* meanings of "circumstantial evidence." The findings would, I think, be worrisome (though, going by peculiar acquittals in certain recent publicized trials, English as well as American, perhaps no more so than many jurors' notions of how *un*reasonable "a reasonable doubt" has to be before they will feel forced to join any sensible colleagues in voting for a verdict of Guilty).

East of New Iberia I saw the first of several "cities of the dead," cemeteries in which the graves are above the often-waterlogged ground—an arrangement that would have gone down well with the British Resurrectionists, who dug up fairly fresh corpses for retail to schools of anatomy till an act of 1832, "the Surgeons' Charter," put them out of business by permitting "persons having lawful possession" of bodies to pass them on to accredited anatomists.

In the early evening, getting close to my destination of New Orleans, the train crossed the Mississippi on the bridge, four and a half miles long, that is unintendedly aptly named after Huey P. Long, the crime-financed "Kingfish" of Louisiana politics, first as governor and then as a U.S. senator, who was shot to death by a young doctor, Carl Weiss, in the state capitol at Baton Rouge in September 1935. Weiss was himself shot to death—excessively, with sixty-one bullets—by Long's failed bodyguards. There are revisionist theories that Long was not killed by Weiss but by one of the bodyguards, the rest of them then lying to protect their colleague; but, in common with virtually all assassination theorists, those who have concocted revised versions of the Long case have not allowed truths to interfere with their guesswork.

Speaking more generally of spurious solvers of unsolved crimes, it would be beneficial if some of them would understand the simple fact, so simple that it is usually overlooked, that murder mysteries, unlike crosswords or conundrums, are not *intended* to be solved. Far too often with such persons ("Ripperology" is stuffed with them, has been disgraced by them), a desperate hope of solving an insoluble mystery becomes a determination to *seem* to have solved it, never minding how many lies need to be told toward that end, and relying on the first two components of Lincoln's (or was it P. T. Barnum's?) fooling-the-people dictum.

My hotel in New Orleans was the Pontchartrain, which is on St. Charles Avenue in the Garden District. It had been recommended to me, and now I shall recommend it too. Few city hotels can be called charming, but that word is appropriate to the Pontchartrain. Much of the charm is made by the visible employees, who are carefully chosen and well trained. During my only full day there, the reception clerks, whom I had not seen since I had booked in, greeted me by name, and the waitress in the Bayou Bar, remembering me from the night before, said, "Dewar's and Schweppes ginger ale, right?"

According to the hotel's publicity, each of the hundred guest rooms is decorated in a different way. Mine was pretty and had framed copies of Redouté roses on the walls (making me feel at home, for I have some of those in my own bedroom). The taps in the bathroom were wonderfully uncomplicated. In America one needs an honors degree in sanitary fittings so as to understand the umpteen gadgets: taps that don't turn but have to be pushed or pulled, taps in the form of levers or push buttons, flushes worked by disguised pedals on the floor, bath and basin plugs operated by remote control—and, most bewildering of all, consoles of dials and things at the feet end of baths, which also work the showers. I usually get into an empty bath and then turn the water on, and twice during this trip I touched the wrong knob and got completely drenched.

At breakfast in the Café Pontchartrain, eavesdropping on the people at the next table, I heard a young woman expressing concern that her father had Alzheimer's Disease, for he had given up showering, and when asked why he had stopped had said that he couldn't figure out how the shower worked. I wondered whether I should try to reassure her, but by the time I decided that I should, the conversation had moved from one health subject to another, problems occasioned by erratic bowel movements. Having enjoyed my breakfast till then, I settled my bill and left.

I boarded one of the olive-green trolleys that run along the center of St. Charles Avenue to the intersecting Canal Street, the main street of New Orleans, the southern stretch of which is the western side of the French Quarter. The St. Charles Avenue Streetcar Line, dating from 1835, is the only one left in the city; there is no longer a Streetcar Named Desire. The French Quarter, a crisscrossing of narrow streets, many with ornate buildings, is more French looking than any part of France I have seen; perhaps that is due to the paradox that most of the architecture isn't French at all but Spanish.

I spent much of the morning at the Historic New Orleans Collection, reading books and newspaper cuttings and comparing a new map of the city with old ones, and then walked through to the parallel street, Bourbon, and went into the Old Absinthe House, which is prefixed "Jean Lafitte's," though there doesn't seem to be an ounce of evidence that that privateer of the early nineteenth century ever even entered the place, which was then a kind of corner grocery shop of goods imported from Spain. The walls of the barroom are practically hidden behind a patchwork of customers' visiting cards; lamps hanging over the circular counter are shaded with football helmets in the black and gold colors of the local team, the Saints.

Less than enamored of the décor, I thought of walking out when the barmaid said she couldn't provide ginger ale to go with scotch, suggested Seven-Up instead, and seemed to find my request for a small jug of tap water hard to comply with but decided to stay as I needed somewhere to sit while looking through notes I had made and photocopies I had been given, all to do with the Kate Townsend story.

That wasn't her real name. Born in England in 1839, the daughter of a stevedore on the Liverpool docks, she was seventeen when she abandoned her illegitimate children, fathered by a sailor she had got to know after using a pewter mug to knock out two ruffians who had attacked him in the dancehall where she worked as a barmaid, and emigrated to America, to New Orleans—more specifically, to the red-light district in and on both sides of the northern part of Canal Street.

Handsome and voluptuous, she was an overnight success as a prostitute. She moved from one brothel to another, and, wherever she went, her satisfied clients were sure to follow. She was thrifty as well as busy, and after six years had sufficient capital to open a brothel of her own on Villere Street, attracting standing-room-only business from the start. A pioneer of sorts, she enlisted financial and string-pulling assistance from politicians and city officials with whom she was on intimate terms and built a bespoke pleasure dome, three stories high, at 40 Basin Street. (I had thought of trying to find the site but had decided not to, partly because I, a duffer at arithmetic, had been perplexed by the renumberings of the buildings along Basin Street—but chiefly, I gladly admit, because people I had spoken to at the historical collection had put the wind up me by saying that no one in his right mind would walk alone in an area where so few strangers walked alone that anyone who did was likely to be mugged more than once.)

Having created the most opulent brothel in the country, perhaps in the world, Kate Townsend recruited prostitutes befitting the premises and ruled them with a rod of iron, insisting that, whatever the time of day, they wear full evening dress between assignments, levying fines for what she considered to be breaches of social or professional behavior, and firing any girl found guilty of moonlighting on her one day off during the week.

She was as strict with regard to the clientele, personally vetting the credentials of first-time callers, refusing admission to regulars till they had settled overdue charge accounts, and, herself acting as bouncer, evicting clients who had broken her rules of gentlemanly conduct.

In the early years of the establishment, she occasionally took time off from her proprietorial duties to extend personal service to particularly valued clients, charging fifty dollars an hour, far more than double her subcontractual rate, for the pleasure of her company in her boudoir on the ground floor, which would subsequently be described by the *New Orleans Picayune:*

In the left-hand corner was a magnificent *étagère* [whatnot], upon which were statuettes, the work of renowned artists, and small articles of vertu, betraying good taste, both in selection and arrangement. A finely carved though small marble table stood next, while adjoining this was a splendid glass-door *armoire,* on the shelves of which were stored a plethora of the finest linen wear and bed clothing. Next the *armoire* was a rep and damask sofa, and over the mantel was a costly French mirror with gilt frame. A large sideboard stood in the corner next a window on the other side of the chimney, and in this was stored a large quantity of silverware. Another *armoire* similar to the one just described, a table, and a bed completed the furniture of the room, saving the arm-chairs, of which there were quite a number, covered with rep and damask, with tête-à-têtes to match. The hangings of the bed, even the mosquito bar, were of lace, and an exquisite basket of flowers hung suspended from the tester of the bed. Around the walls were suspended chaste and costly oil paintings.

As the years passed, Kate's body expanded, becoming voluminous rather than voluptuous; she eventually tipped the scales at over three hundred pounds. A local paper, the *States,* noted that her enormity "attracted general attention on the street" and that her bust "never failed to provoke astonishment in those who chanced to meet her." Perhaps coincidentally, the more her weight increased, the more irascible she became.

Since shortly after her arrival in the city she had known, at first professionally, a man of about her own age, Treville Egbert Sykes, for an obvious reason known as Bill, who was the black sheep of a respectable New Orleans family. In 1878 he became the first and only male resident of 40 Basin Street, getting bed, board, and miscellaneous fringe benefits in exchange for attracting custom, keeping the accounts, and doing odd jobs about the brothel.

The arrangement got off to a bad start. He had hardly settled in when Kate had him arrested, claiming that he had forged her signature on checks totaling seven thousand dollars; soon afterward, however, she withdrew the complaint. From then on, according to his story (much of which was corroborated), she led him "a dogs life," refusing to pay him the pocket money she had promised, beating him, locking him in cupboards, once cutting his nose almost off with a slash of the bowie knife she always kept in her reticule (the weapon, which had been used by one card sharper to kill another, was a present to her from a policeman client), and every so often prodding him with the knife and remarking that she felt like "opening his belly."

Even so, Sykes stayed with her for five years. But for a specially violent rumpus, he, seemingly the soul of complaisance, would almost surely have stayed longer.

By October 1883 his position as her "fancy man" was undermined by her increasing affection toward a young gigolo named McLern. When she began expressing her affection by inviting McLern into her boudoir on a complimentary basis, Sykes protested—and, while the resting girls looked on, received a beating from Kate, assisted by McLern.

Next day, while the head girl, Molly Johnson, was in the kitchen, Kate waddled in, picked up a butcher's knife and began shadow fencing with it, screaming, "I've a good mind to take this and open Sykes's belly!" Although apprehensive of the safety of her own digestive organs, Molly put in a good word for Sykes and then, believing that Kate had exhausted both herself and her lethal inclination, took the butcher's knife from her and called Sykes into the kitchen—whereupon Kate, having got some of her breath back, belabored him with a breadboard while using her free hand to rip his clothes, stopping only when he fell to the floor, beyond her bending ability, and slithered on his hands and knees from the kitchen.

An hour or so later, Molly encountered Kate on the stairs leading to, among other top-floor rooms, Sykes's. Seeing her there was itself unusual, for her excessive weight had made climbing only a few steps arduous, requiring a breathtaking pause for recovery. Adding menace to the unusualness, she was brandishing the butcher's knife. Between pants, Kate explained to Molly, "I came up to open Sykes's belly—I can't find him—I'll kill him yet." Molly persuaded her to descend to the ground floor.

On the night of Thursday, November 1, Kate, Molly, McLern, and a crony of his got drunk on champagne in a nearby café, Pizzini's. Kate and McLern had a tiff. He threatened to hit her with a bottle but immediately said he was only joking when she produced the bowie knife from her reticule. Apparently disappointed by his submission, she stropped the knife on the palm of her free hand and murmured wistfully, "I've got to cut somebody." Then, undoubtedly to the relief of everybody within range of her, she particularized her hankering, declaring, "I know—I'll go home and open Sykes's belly."

It appears that neither of the male members of the party accompanied the women back to the brothel. As soon as Kate had shambled into her boudoir, Molly, who seems to have been quite a nice girl in at least one respect, warned Sykes to lock and bar his door. The next day and that night Kate stayed in bed, recovering from her hangover.

At about half past nine on Saturday morning, Sykes went in to see her. After a minute or so, there were screams, shouts, and thuds. The black housekeeper, graced with the name of Mary Philomena, opened the door and saw Kate and Sykes scrapping near the bed. While she was still wondering whether or not to interfere, Sykes pushed her back into the hall and locked the door.

Silence for a moment, then a dreadful medley of sounds, then silence again.

The door opened. Sykes appeared. His clothes were in tatters; he was bleeding from cuts on his left side, near his breast and above his knee.

"Well, Mary," he remarked, punctiliously closing the door behind him, "Kate's gone."

"What you's done, Mr. Sykes?" the housekeeper enquired.

He shrugged. "I had to do it," he said, speaking, it seems, in the don't-ask-silly-questions way that George Leigh Mallory did in replying, "Because it is there," when asked why he was so keen to conquer Mount Everest. Adding nothing to his slight explanation, Sykes started to limp up the stairs.

What follows is a piecing together of parts of reports in various editions of several newspapers:

> The affrighted cook, Rose Garcia, joined the housekeeper, and for a few seconds they gazed at the bloodstained man slowly proceeding to his room. Then shriek after shriek went up from the two terrified women, and soon a number of the inmates and neighbors were there. With trembling hands, they opened the door, and one glance sufficed to reveal the fate of Kate Townsend, who reigned queen of the frail sisterhood of the demi-mondaine for many years, and who was probably known in every quarter of the land. The inordinately stout mistress of the house was lying across the bed, her chemise torn and bloodstained, her bare feet yet standing on the floor, dipped in a pool of blood which darkened the crimson hue which prevailed in the pattern of the costly velvet carpet.

With a faint hope of bringing back to life the inanimate form, those present began chafing her bloodstained hands and feet with ice water and whiskey, but their efforts were in vain.

Officers Clarke and Hormle heard the uproar, and, thinking it was the same old fight between Sykes and Townsend, went to the scene. Clarke rushed out in search of a physician, and hailed Dr. Venzie, who was passing in his buggy on his way to the hospital. On looking at the deceased, the doctor said: "That woman has been dead too long to talk about."

The officer who had instituted a search for the weapon looked through the open window into the yard and saw a bowie knife, about nine inches long; another bloodstained implement, a pair of pruning shears that Miss Kate had used to trim plants in the yard, was lying nearby. When the bloody weapons were held up to the vast crowds of curious people who had gathered on the sidewalk, a cry of horror came from the females present.

Surmising who had committed the deed, Officer Clarke ran upstairs in search of Sykes, whom he found in his room. Sykes had changed his clothing and donned a pair of gray pants, black coat and hat. Saying, "I'm going to give myself up," he surrendered, and the officer conducted him to the Central Station and made affidavit against him.

At 40 Basin Street, the large hall and elegantly furnished rooms were crowded with eager spectators, females as well as men, who hoped to witness the autopsy, and when the Coroner arrived, the officers had considerable difficulty in clearing the room in which the gory corpse lay on the beautifully carved bed, with its costly hangings and trimmings, now all stained with blood. A sheet thrown over the form hid the face from view, but when that was lifted, the deed in all its shocking reality was revealed.

There were shrill barks from under the bed, and a diminutive black-and-tan dog darted forth to drive away the curious crowd. It was Miss Kate's pet, and the animal, faithful even in death, remained by its mistress's side and refused to be moved. Finally the dainty little animal was captured and conveyed to a room upstairs, all the while giving voice to its evident desire to be with its dead friend.

The Townsend murder case as a "cartoon strip" in a nineteenth-century newspaper.

A jury of five men was impaneled. No persons besides the jurors, reporters and two officers witnessed the autopsy. When the doctors cut Miss Kate open, the fat was seen to be six inches in thickness. The examination revealed eleven wounds, three of which were fatal, and the jury brought in a verdict of death from hemorrhage, the result of punctured wounds of the left lung, heart and large blood vessels. After the inquest was concluded, preparations were made to array the body for the grave.

The funeral was on November 5 (Guy Fawkes Day in England). The furniture in the brothel was draped with white silk rather than the usual linen or muslin. In accordance with Kate Townsend's pre-mortem wish, champagne was served to the guests. The hearse was followed to

Metarie Cemetery by a procession of twenty carriages. There were no men among the visible mourners.

Treville Sykes was acquitted of murder, the jury having accepted his plea of self-defense. He then produced a will, made in 1873, five years before he had become a full-timer at the brothel, in which Kate Townsend had bequeathed him all of her worldly goods. After five years of legalistic wrangling, mostly to do with a state law that was intended to deter couples from living in open concubinage, Sykes's share of the estate amounted to precisely thirty-four dollars.

While the lawyers had been prospering at his expense, Molly Johnson had taken over the brothel. She continued to run it till her untimely death in 1889, when the effects were auctioned. For some years afterward, the building, determinedly expunged of all signs of its previous purpose, was the local headquarters of the entirely male society of Elks.

Just as I was gathering my Kate Townsend notes together, the Old Absinthe House, quiet till then, was made noisy owing to the arrival of a large elderly man and two dainty young women at the part of the counter to the left of where I was perched. The man was almost entirely gray: his suit and tie matched his gray hair, and his complexion was gray as well. The grayness was accentuated by his companions, who pressed against him, one each side, like bookends; the girl on his right was Spanish looking and was dressed in glossy black, the other was blonde and was wearing a pink suit and ornately framed spectacles.

Myself excepted, everyone in the bar recognized the gray man and called out, "Hi, John," and he gave the impression that he recognized each of them, saying, "How y'doing?" or "Long time" or "Y're looking well," though without adding a name to the greeting. I asked the man on my right who the celebrity was and was told, in a tone of wonderment that I didn't know, that he was a former governor of Louisiana: "A real good old boy . . . one hell of an improvement on Huey P. Long and his brother Earl."

I had asked my brief question quietly, but the politician had heard me. He said, "Ah heard yo accent, suh, and assoom—pray correct me if ah'm mistaken—that y're from Inglund." Even before I had nodded, the blonde girl said, "Inglund—imagine," and the dark girl, not to be outdone, said, "Cute, real cute."

The politician continued talking to me. He gazed intently in my direction but seemed to be looking not at my face but at something far more interesting on the wall behind. I presumed that his remarks were amusing—no more than presumed because the girls, who must either have heard the remarks before or have taken it for granted that everything he said was side-splitting, both started roaring with laughter before he got to the end of any remark, making the rest inaudible. It was like listening to a string of those crossword clues that have words missing from quotations. As I didn't want him, never mind them, to think that I had no sense of humor, I fixed a smirk on my face, a kind of *rictus sardonicus,* meanwhile hoping that the girls had got it right and he had not started talking about something tragic. I was quite relieved when he and they, still conscientiously flanking him, left.

I popped into an adjacent restaurant for a quick but filling lunch of gumbo fish-and-chicken soup and bread-and-butter pudding, then strolled out of the French Quarter to Lafayette Square, which I found to be very pleasant indeed. Unlike most squares in London (or for that matter, Manhattan), it really is square. There are modern white buildings, none too tall, on three sides, and the white background both sharpens the silhouettes of the many trees and seems to darken the green of the trees, the well-kept lawns, and the privet hedges bordering some of the neat paths. The square must look lovely at night, when the old-fashioned lamps are lit. At the center, facing the main street, is a statue of Henry Clay, the politician of the first half of the nineteenth century who, from his efforts to hold the Union together in the face of the issue of slavery, became known as the Great Pacificator. The statue, which used to stand at the crossing of Canal and Royal streets (I suppose it was moved from there because it was contributing to traffic jams), seems to be the only thing left in New Orleans that is associated with the murder, in 1890, of the city's chief of police, David Hennessey.

One of the several mysteries of that case is the fact that Hennessey *was* the chief of police. When he was appointed in 1888, at the age of twenty-nine, the record of his police career was drab apart from a single achievement seven years before—and that achievement had been nullified by a subsequent act.

In the summer of 1881 Hennessey and his cousin Michael, who was also a member of the police force, assisted in the arrest of Giuseppe

Esposito, a Sicilian criminal living in New Orleans who was suspected of having created the first Mafia gang in America; deported in secret, for fear that members of his gang would try to effect his escape, Esposito was found guilty of eighteen murders and a hundred kidnappings in Sicily but was spared the death sentence through the intervention of the king of Italy, who seems to have been the original Royal Jelly. In the autumn of 1881 Michael Hennessey, while drunk, assaulted a man in Kate Townsend's brothel at 40 Basin Street, created a disturbance at another brothel in the vicinity, and was charged by Thomas Devereaux, the chief of detectives, with conduct unbecoming an officer. Incensed by such discipline, the Hennessey cousins ambushed the chief. As Michael and Devereaux began firing shots at each other, David crept up behind the chief and put a bullet through his head.

When both of the cousins were acquitted of any crime, the *New Orleans States* commented: "We are astounded that a jury in a Christian and enlightened country would return such a verdict as 'not guilty' in this case. . . . Not even the savage tribes of the western plains would recognize such a mode of seeking protection or revenge as the Hennesseys resorted to when they murdered Thomas Devereaux, for even savages will not tolerate assassination; and all the facts proved, beyond question, that this was a deliberate and bloody assassination." A year or so later, Michael Hennessey moved to Texas, eventually to Houston, where in 1886 he was shot dead by some unknown person.

By the time David Hennessey was put in charge of the New Orleans police, the number of Italians living in the city had risen to about thirty thousand, making them the largest white-minority population. The number of crimes attributed to, though rarely proved against, Italians was vastly out of proportion to the number of Italian residents. The only action Hennessey seems to have taken in that regard was to call gang leaders together and plead with them to restrict their activities to within their own communities and to curb the enmity between them.

In May 1890 members of one gang fired a fusillade of bullets at the wagon in which members of another gang, the Mantrangas, were traveling from the part of the docks where they had taken over the contract for the employment of stevedores. Largely on the basis of evidence from the Mantrangas, members of the Provenzano gang were charged with the attack. The Mantrangas hired a lawyer and a private detective to help the district attorney. Rightly or wrongly, the Mantrangas believed that Hennessey was financially beholden to the Provenzanos, and that suspicion was strengthened when, at the trial, the police furnished no witnesses for the prosecution, while officers attempted to provide alibis for some of the defendants. The Provenzanos were convicted, but a new lawyer employed on their behalf won a retrial. The Mantrangas' private detective informed them that Hennessey had brought in the new lawyer.

At eleven o'clock on the rainy night of Wednesday, October 15, two days before the retrial, Hennessey left his headquarters with a friend, William O'Connor, who was a captain in one of the armed private-police forces that patrolled parts of the city. After eating oysters in a saloon on Rampart Street, the northern edge of the French Quarter, they walked onto the corner of Girod Street, where they parted, Hennessey walking toward his home at 275 Girod, between Basin and Franklin streets. He was almost there when there was the sound of a whistle—a long note, three short ones, the long note repeated.

A signal.

Half a dozen men emerged from doorways, firing shotguns at Hennessey. Six shots hit their target, but as the men ran off in different directions, Hennessey, still standing, loosed off his revolver—and continued pulling the trigger when the gun was empty, even after he had fallen in the mud.

Hearing the explosions, O'Connor raced to the scene. He afterward told reporters: "Bending over the chief, I said to him, 'Who gave it to you, Dave?' He replied, 'Put your ear down here.' As I bent down again, he whispered the word 'Dagoes.'"

Hennessey died in hospital the next morning. He remained conscious till near the end but—never minding that he was the chief of police—refused to answer questions. "I'm not going to die," he said. "Those people can't kill me. God is good, and I will get well."

In England the word *dago* (which sounds rude but isn't, for it is simply a corruption of the common Spanish name Diego), is applied mainly to persons of Spanish or Portuguese origin. But in New Orleans, apparently, at least at the time of the murder of David Hennessey, the word was applied only to Italians. At any rate, even before Hennessey was dead, the mayor, Joseph Shakspeare (that is not a misprint), ordered the police to scour the Italian neighborhood, saying, "Arrest every Italian you come across, if necessary." He also provided further city funds to the Committee of Fifty, composed of prominent businessmen, which he had recently set up to investigate the activities of secret societies, particularly the one or several known as the Mafia, whose membership seemed to be restricted to Sicilians.

Different reports give different reckonings of the number of Italians who, being Italian, were arrested for questioning in connection with the murder; but of however many it actually was, nineteen—all more-specifically Sicilian, most of them members or known associates of the Mantranga gang—were indicted either as direct participants in the shooting or as accessories before the fact. The trial was delayed until after the delayed retrial of the Provenzanos, all of whom were this time acquitted. Interestingly, counsel who had assisted the district attorney in the prosecution of the Provenzanos became defense lawyers in the Hennessey case, while those who had defended the Provenzanos joined in the prosecution at the murder trial.

The courthouse, which was on Lafayette Square, looked magnificent from the outside, being of baroque design, built of yellow bricks, but the interior areas around the courtroom were unkempt, described by a reporter as "a colossal spittoon . . . filthy in the extreme. . . . The atmosphere of the place was scarcely fit to be breathed by human beings, and the incessant hum of voices of the loungers penetrated even to the tribunal of justice itself."

On the first day of the trial, the judge accepted the district attorney's submission that the defendants should be split into two groups, nine to be tried at once, the remaining ten at a later date.

No one seems to have wanted to serve on the jury. Thirteen hundred veniremen managed to escape selection through a variety of swearings: opposition to capital punishment, doubt (yes, even then) as to the value of circumstantial evidence, prejudice against Sicilians, belief that no Sicilian could possibly be guilty of even the slightest of crimes.

At last, after eleven days, the jury box was filled, and the trial really began. The prosecution, in trying to prove a Mafia conspiracy, made much of the part Hennessey had played in the arrest of Giuseppe Esposito; witnesses were called who claimed to have seen one or another of the defendants loitering near Hennessey's home shortly before the attack or running from the scene immediately afterward; other prosecution witnesses claimed to have heard one or more of the defendants speaking of the attack as if with guilty knowledge of it. The defense called witnesses in aid of alibis and poured scorn on the prosecution's eye- and ear-witness evidence.

On Friday the Thirteenth, March 1891, the jury acquitted six of the defendants and declared themselves unable to reach a verdict as to the other three. Since further charges were pending against all nine men, they were returned to the Parish Prison, which was at the intersection of Orleans and Treme streets, close to what is now Louis Armstrong Park. News of the result had spread through the city, and the route of the Black Maria was thronged with angry demonstrators chanting words that had become a mordant catchphrase: "Who Killa de Chief?" That night, sixty-one businessmen signed a notice for publication in the local papers next morning: "All good citizens are invited to attend a mass meeting on Saturday, 14 March, at 10 o'clock A.M., at Clay Statue, to take steps to remedy the failure of justice in the Hennessey case. Come prepared for action."

Thousands accepted the invitation. They received complimentary copies of a special edition of the *States*, the front page of which was devoted to the Hennessey case:

New Orleans is become the haven of murderers and the safe vantage ground for the Sicilian Mafia and their hired agents of American birth, who murder officers of the law, and who buy jurors and suborn witnesses, under the hooded eyes of blind justice. . . .

Rise, outraged people of New Orleans! Let those who have attempted to sap the very foundations of your Temples of Justice be in one vengeful hour swept from your midst. Peaceably if you can, forcibly if you must!

Three of the men who had signed the notice stood on the pedestal of the Clay statue and, one after another, addressed the crowd. The last to speak, to shout above the growing clamor, was a lawyer, William Parkerson, who had managed the election campaign of Mayor Shakspeare (who was presently incommunicado at his club, the Pickwick). If any policemen had been sent to control the gathering, their presence went unnoticed—and none was seen on the streets as the crowd that had become a mob swept toward the prison—and none was seen in the vicinity of the prison as the thirty armed men at the head of the mob, Parkerson among them, tried to break down the main door. Failing, the vigilantes turned their attention to a less substantial side door on Treme Street. Inside the prison, the Sicilians were released from their cells, told to seek hiding places. As the door broke, Parkerson shouted, "Only men with guns go in." His order was obeyed.

Within a short while, certainly no more than half an hour, what seems to have been the worst mass lynching in American history had taken place. Ten of the Sicilian prisoners had been shot to death; one other had been hanged. Three were of the six who had been found not guilty of the murder of David Hennessey, three were those who had been ordered to be retried for the murder, as the jury had been unable to decide on their guilt or innocence, and five were of the ten who were awaiting trial for the murder.

Presumably because it was felt that the survivors among the untried group had suffered more than enough during the break-in, the intended second trial was called off; also, the charges pending against the three acquitted defendants were dropped. Less understandably, no charge, not even for causing damage to the fabric of the Parish Prison, was brought against Colonel Parkerson or any other of the men who now boasted that they had "given the dagoes a lesson in justice."

The lynchings caused a crisis in diplomatic relations between Italy and the United States. The Italian ambassador was withdrawn; there was even talk of war. Relations were not fully restored till President Benjamin Harrison, going against the wishes of Congress, paid the Italian government an indemnity of $25,000 from a fund that was available to him for "unforeseen emergencies."

Before 1891 comparatively few Americans outside New Orleans had heard the word *mafia*. Press coverage of the lynchings, of the ostensible reason for them, did not merely put the word into common parlance but created a wave of fear that Sicilians, not so much immigrants as fugitives, had formed a *national* criminal conspiracy; a survey of papers with large circulations showed that nearly half believed that the lynchings had been in a good cause—that the means were appropriate to the end, which was to reduce the power of the New Orleans "branch" of *The* Mafia. It is hard to understand how the approving editorialists conjured the notion of a nationwide affiliation of gangs from the Hennessey case. If Hennessey was murdered by Sicilians, then the reason for the crime, almost certainly, was that one gang of Sicilians suspected that he was in the pay of another gang of Sicilians, their deadly enemies—most peculiar "proof" of what in England is known as "the old pals act." One of the editorialists declared that the fact that "the secret organization styled 'Mafia' exists [is] supported by the long record of blood-curdling crimes, it being almost impossible to discover the perpetrators or to secure witnesses"—in other words, an absence of evidence was the best evidence of all.

During the century or so since the Hennessey case, the belief that all gangs of Italian American criminals belong to a vast Mafia cartel has become the accepted view—fostered by law-enforcement agencies, glad of any excuse for their failure as gangbusters; by the gangs themselves, which use terms like the Syndicate and the Mob so as to frighten prospective or recalcitrant victims; and by imaginative reporters and opportunistic politicians. In the early 1950s Estes Kefauver, chairman of the Senate Crime Investigation Committee, claimed, without an ounce of proof, that a national Mafia had been uncovered; later in the same decade a gathering of gang leaders at the home of one of them in Apalachin was accidentally disturbed by New York state policemen, and an evidenceless surmise that the gangsters were members of "The Mafia Grand Council" was immediately taken as gospel; more recently, confused and often contradictory tales from so-called supergrasses, all menial gangsters (one of them, Joseph Valachi, coming up with a new name for the Mafia: Cosa Nostra), have been subedited by authors and ghostwriters whose contracts were negotiated on the understanding that the finished works would support the notion of a national Mafia. If it were not for the impossibility of proving a negative in such matters, I would go farther than saying that the notion of *one* Mafia is rather hard to credit.

I had not intended to spend the rest of the afternoon on the prettified stretch of riverfront at the foot of Canal Street but so enjoyed the sights, showboats especially, that I did. I had thought of spending the evening at Preservation Hall, listening to jazz, but was put off from that, partly because I had been told that I would need to queue to get in, partly because during the day I had heard so many fragments of jazz played by buskers, partly because the word "jazz" is too often used nowadays as an excuse for the musical equivalent of "conceptual art," and mainly because I knew that popular music, some of it traditional jazz, was played in the Pontchartrain's Bayou Bar by the Johnnie Bachemin Trio.

I went into the bar early enough to get the table farthest from the bandstand, was served drinks by the waitress who remembered what I drank, and had an unconventional but enjoyable dinner, taking my time between the courses: a plateful of oysters prepared in different ways (Bienville, with mushrooms and shrimps; Creole, with chopped tomatoes; Lafayette, with crabmeat), a Caesar salad, and something called a mile-high pie, mostly a mingling of ice creams, from which I withdrew after no more than a couple of furlongs.

I waited till the musicians were between sets before I made to leave, then thanked them, not out of politeness but because I really had liked the tunes they had played and the uncomplicated way in which they had played them. Too often, musical arrangements seem intended to hide the melodies, and I am reminded of the criticism that is supposed to have been made by a royal patron of Antonio Salieri to the composer Salieri surely did not murder: "Too many notes, Mozart."

9

To Atlanta

I t was still dark when I was driven to the station to catch the seven o'clock train on the Crescent route to Atlanta. The cabbie, who was white, was probably even older than my wonderful Hurshell in Chicago. I asked him how long he had been driving for a living, and he said: "Forty-nine years. I'll clock fifty, then I'll call it a day."

On all of the previous trains, black passengers had been outnumbered by black staff (and I hadn't seen a single black guest in any of the hotels), but there were many black passengers on this one. Most of them, I learned before boarding, were supporters of the New Orleans Saints football team traveling to Atlanta for an important match against that city's team, the Falcons. Their behavior was refined compared with that of English lager-louts who use our kind of football as an excuse for hooliganism, but some of the things they shouted made the forthcoming game sound like a small religious war: "We'll leave them D-E-D dead" . . . "Complete annihilation that's what" . . . "[the Saints' tailback, whose name escaped me] is gonna demolish them birds."

The first fifteen miles of the journey must be somewhat alarming on gusty days, for the track extends across Lake Pontchartrain on a causeway that looks insufficiently wider than the track itself, with the western shore out of sight most of the time and the eastern one only a fuzzy streak. There are many swamps, some with tall, vividly green trees, in the remaining bit of Louisiana on the far side of the lake; but from near the start of Mississippi, the land starts to dry out, and the train passes through dense forests.

I know that the town of Laurel, one of the four stopping places in Mississippi, began as a lumber camp, and I suppose it was named after the tree. I have found out how the other places came by their names. When Picayune was incorporated as a township at the start of the twentieth century, it was given that name by the wealthiest resident, whose husband ran the New Orleans daily paper, the *Picayune* (now merged with the *Times*), which was called that because it sold for a nickel, a coin known locally as a picayune. Hattiesburg was founded by a lumberman whose wife's name was Hattie. Meridian was christened by railroad developers who thought the word meant "junction."

By lunchtime (*my* lunchtime; I went to the last, uncrowded sitting), the train had departed from Birmingham, Alabama, on both sides of which, and on both sides of the tracks, were lines of inhabited shanties, some satirically flying the Stars and Stripes. When I reached the observation car on the way back to my seat, I was surprised by what I saw and heard. A slim young black woman standing at one end was thunderously reciting a poem, something about the scent of roses, to the people sitting there, several of whom were holding copies of a small paperback book of verse that the reciter had presumably sold to them.

The next stop, the last before Atlanta, was Anniston, which I had heard of in connection with Stanford White, one of the eastern architects who in the 1880s were hired by the owners of the local textile mills and blast furnaces to fashion Anniston as a "model town."

When I went to the café a little while later, the only passenger there was the performing poet. I introduced myself, saying that I too was a writer, that the first book I had published was a collection of verse, and she gave me a business card that read, "HAVE POEMS, WILL TRAVEL" above the offer of "poetry recitals for church functions, juvenile halls, jails, luncheons and banquets, weddings, fashion shows, family reunions, and various events." We talked pleasantly enough till I happened to mention that I wrote about true crime, and she, I hope not realizing that she was being rude, said: "Oh, in that case we have nothing in common. I am a Christian poet, so I would not think of writing anything sordid, in opposition to the teaching of our Lord. My purpose is to uplift."

Well, that irritated me. Trying, though not hard, to sound affable, I pointed out (*a*) that the Bible contains a good many crime stories, including some about murder, starting in the fourth chapter of the Book of Genesis with the case of Cain and Abel, (*b*) that several undoubtedly devout Christians (including clergymen, George A. Birmingham, Evelyn Burnaby, and John Rowland among them) had made worthwhile contributions to the true-crime genre, (*c*) that some rather good poets (Shakespeare, Browning, Housman, for instance) had considered murder a perfectly fit subject for poetry, and—only because I could tell that my little impromptu lecture was falling on determinedly deaf ears—(*d*) that it was all too easy, a variation on adding acid to the lemon, to write poetry on subjects such as the scent of roses, which were poetic to start with. Then, worried for the sake of the performing poet that nothing I had said had upset her, I moved to the part of the café where smoking was legal and smoked a cigarette unenjoyably and, before long, vexedly, because I couldn't for the life of me remember a brief quotation that I had thought I knew word-perfectly: an amused condemnation by P. G. Wodehouse of slighter-than-minor, unfathomable, unpoetic poets who in the 1920s and '30s had their little books bound in "squashy mauve covers" (at least I have that fragment of another Wodehouse quotation right).

Although, excepting *Psmith Journalist*, no really serious crime contributes to the plot of any of his ninety or so mostly wonderful books, Wodehouse took sufficient interest in true crime to be a member of Our Society (called "the crimes club" by people who know no better). When I became honorary secretary of the society, following on from Judge Henry Elam, who had done the job for forty-two years, I reconstructed the records stretching back to 1903. An addendum to the minutes of the meeting on February 25, 1934, notes that Wodehouse did not hear the denouement of the after-dinner talk on a strange case of double murder near Guildford, Surrey, for he "left early, presumably because one or two of the gruesome exhibits proved too much [for him]."

I too am rather squeamish. It is the facts that accrete around murders, not the acts of murder, that engage my interest. Years ago I suggested a Law of Frissonology—*squeamishness increases in inverse relation to the gravity of the cause*—which I exemplified with an experience I had had:

During dinner at the Savage Club, my companion, a forensic pathologist, received a message that he was needed at his mortuary to perform an autopsy on the body of a person who, some five weeks before, had been clumsily murdered with a blunt ax. The pathologist suggested that both of us should repair to the mortuary, he to hack, I to admire his deftness, and then, after he had brushed his nails, return to the club to finish the port. I was unenthusiastic but did not have the courage to demur (a statement that could, but will not, lead me on to a discussion of the equivocal nature of bravery). But the pathologist, through too hurriedly munching a nutty petit-four, broke a tooth. As luck would have it, a colleague of his, an odontologist, was dining at a nearby table. The pathologist called out to him for help, and the odontologist, an indiscriminate enthusiast, said that, if we could bear waiting a few minutes, he would be delighted to drive us to the mortuary—via his house, where, in the garage, he would remove the stump of tooth. The thought of standing idly by during such an extraction in such surroundings—and perhaps, my imagination hinted, with the odontologist using unconventional tools—was harder to stomach than that of observing a month-old corpse being dissected, and so I muttered an excuse for leaving and lurched out into St. James's.

As there were insufficient cabs at Atlanta's Peachtree Station, I shared one with a Louisiana lawyer and his swell-elegant wife, both Saints' fans ("We shall wipe the Falcons out," she told me genteelly—and, as it transpired, with metaphorical accuracy), whose hotel was near mine, the Peachtree Plaza, which is the tallest hotel in America—or was then: building-height records last so fleetingly in this country that the hotel may by now have been overreached by another or others.

My room was on the forty-sixth floor, slightly more than halfway up the cone-shaped building. I had thought that my eyes had become blasé from an extravagance of scenery during my present travels, but they were astounded by the nighttime view through the window, which was the entire outside wall of the room. As I suffer from vertigo, sometimes to the hallucinatory extent of glimpses of Kim Novak, I never ventured close enough to the window to be able, if I had had the additional courage, to look down at the dots and dashes of people and vehicles in the street. Proving that logic is no cure for vertigo, the minute I convinced myself that the safety glass really was safe, I intentionally remembered what the Cleveland detective Nate Sowa had said about the "sweet spots" that make car windows unsafe.

I had had very good food in all of the previous hotels, but my meals at the Peachtree Plaza, where I stayed for three days, were the best of all. There is a lingering ignorant snobbishness about food, exemplified by la-di-da persons who, often on the frail basis of one package-deal weekend in Paris, insist that French food (no, if it's French, it has to be cuisine) is the sublimest, or some other hyperbolic word. All I can say is that some of the worst meals I have paid over the odds for were served in French restaurants: restaurants in France, I mean—some of the best meals as well, but that doesn't make the nationalistic generalization less silly. Yet I have never had memorably disgusting food in an American restaurant—and, assisting the flow of my digestive juices, the cost of eating out over here is far less than in England.

I always dined at the same table in the Peachtree Plaza's main restaurant, far enough from the pianist and violinist to enjoy their juxtapositions of Vivaldi with Gershwin, Joplin with Bach, and each time was served by the same waiters, one called Nelson, the other Orlando—names, I supposed, that their respective parents had associated with South Africa and Disneyland rather than with Trafalgar and the Forest of Arden.

I believe that even someone with a good sense of direction, which I don't have, would be confused by Atlanta, which is as higgledy-piggledy as an English city. Hardly any of the blocks run parallel or at right angles with nearby ones, and, so far as I could make out from people I asked who professed to be less baffled than I was, whereas there was no area described as Midtown, several, including a couple that seemed to be in the center, were described as Downtown. The busiest crosstown thoroughfare, called North Avenue on its westward stretch, cuts across the longest street—which, like nearly forty other streets in Atlanta, is called Peachtree.

Of the several explanations I heard as to why the name Peachtree is so bewilderingly ubiquitous, the one that seemed least unlikely was that in the 1830s, when Atlanta was founded (as a railroad settlement, known at first as Terminus and then as Marthasville, vicariously honoring the governor of Georgia, a Goldsmithianly named Mr. Lumpkin, who had a daughter named Martha), there was a trail linking the settlement with an Indian trading post called Standing Peachtree.

One morning I went out by bus to the Atlanta Historical Society, whose several premises, including a beautiful Palladian house, stand in acres of woodland in Buckhead, a northern part of the city, and stayed there hours longer than I had intended to, looking through some of the many boxes of documents relating to the Leo Frank case. Another time I pottered around the Five Points intersection of roads in the center of the city (the site of the original railroad settlement), trying to work out where the National Pencil Company's factory used to be— and at last concluding that it must have been replaced by an ugly brown building belonging to Rich's Bakery at the corner of South Forsyth Street and Martin Luther King Junior Drive (which, if I'm right, used to be Hunter Street; I asked about that at the "Special Operations" police station in the basement of the brown building but did not pursue the question after one of the young officers at the desk, neither of whom could find a street plan, insisted that "MLK Drive ain't never been nothing else," and his colleague agreed with him).

I spent most of another day in the small town of Marietta, on the high ground to the northwest of Atlanta. Having been given directions at the visitors' center, which is in the long-disused train depot, I wandered around the parts of Marietta where there are many lovely old houses—some dating from before the summer of 1864, when, on the outskirts of the town, Sherman's march to Atlanta was briefly halted by Confederate troops led by General Joseph Johnston—and then strolled through Confederate Cemetery to Citizens' Cemetery, where I sat, glad of the shade of tall trees, near a marble headstone that bears a moving, though at first partly inaccurate, inscription:

In this day of fading ideals and disappearing landmarks, little Mary Phagan's heroism is an heirloom than which there is nothing more precious among the old red hills of Georgia.

Sleep, little girl; sleep in your humble grave. But if the angels are good to you in the realms beyond the troubled sunset and the clouded stars, they will let you know that many an aching heart in Georgia beats for you, and many a tear, from eyes unused to weep, has paid you a tribute too sacred for words.

Much has been written about the murder of thirteen-year-old Mary Phagan; but since far too much of the writing has come from propagandists, persons who have decided on the answers before they have asked the questions, the story has been turned into a deceptive fiction. It is to be hoped that someday a diligent researcher with no ax to grind will uncover the truths presently hidden beneath an accumulation of unwarranted assumptions, one-sided slantings, and downright lies. Till then, one cannot even be confident that a bare outline of the story is wholly accurate.

In Georgia April 26 is still observed as Confederate Memorial Day, a state holiday; civil servants are given the option of having the day off or taking another in lieu. Mary Phagan, a pretty dark-haired girl who hailed from Marietta, was murdered at her place of employment, the National Pencil Company, in the early afternoon of April 26, 1913. That was a Saturday. Because of a shortage of the tiny metal strips that it was her job to clip around the erasers on the firm's Magnolia and Jefferson pencils, she had been laid off for a few days.

When she went to the premises, arriving at about noon, she was wearing her best clothes—a lavender-colored dress, trimmed with white lace, and a wide-brimmed blue hat that was decorated with artificial flowers—for she intended to collect the $1.20 that was owed to her and then join the crowds that were already gathering along the nearby stretch of Peachtree Street to watch the parade that would both mourn and celebrate the Confederacy. She must have been positive that, though the factory was closed for the day, the manager would be there.

The manager, Leo Max Frank, was a twenty-nine-year-old Jew. A native of Brooklyn and an engineering graduate of Cornell University, he had run the factory, which was owned by an uncle of his, since 1908. His wife, to whom he had been married for three years, was a member of a wealthy Jewish family in Atlanta. Slim and of less than medium height, he had sleek black hair, prominent eyes that were

Leo Frank, 1913.

made to seem larger by the strong lenses of the spectacles he always wore, and heavy, protruding lips. His appearance was not to his advantage.

He subsequently admitted, without having been pressed, that Mary Phagan came to his office on the Saturday afternoon. He insisted, however, that his only contact with her was when he handed over her paltry pay packet; that even before she left the office, he returned to the paperwork on his desk—that he never saw her again.

Early on the Sunday morning, the night watchman, a black man who was new to the job, went to the basement to use the blacks' toilet and found the body of Mary Phagan lying amid wood shavings, sawdust, and garbage. The body was so dirty that the first policeman to arrive needed to roll down a stocking to tell the color of the skin. Some items of the girl's clothing were missing, as were her silver-mesh purse and the pay packet that she had needed so urgently and that, according to Leo Frank, she had received from him the day before. Several of the remaining garments were torn, and a strip of her underskirt, together with a length of twine, had been used to strangle her. There were cuts and bruises on her head.

Two notes, scrawled in pencil on scraps of yellowed paper, lay near the body. They were not in Mary Phagan's hand, and it seemed that they had been written—and placed—in the hope that the police would believe that she had written them after she was first attacked. Both referred to "a long black Negro," and one read, in part: "Mam that Negro . . . did this. I went to make water and he push me down that hole. . . . I wright while play with me."

A furrowing of the sawdust between the body and a ladder to the ground floor was assumed by the police to mean that the girl, perhaps already dead, had been carried down the ladder and dragged along the ground, but that deduction was amended the next day, following the discovery of bloodstains between a lathe in the "metal room" facing the manager's office and an elevator that went down to the basement.

Almost from the start of the case, the investigators had been suspicious of Leo Frank. Apart from the fact that, so far as was known, he was the last person who had seen Mary Phagan alive, he had been extremely nervous whenever he was interviewed, and he had failed to give a satisfactory explanation as to why, having asked the night watchman to report early on Saturday, he had sent him away till six in the evening—and had phoned him from home an hour later to ask if everything was all right at the factory. The discovery of the bloodstains so close to Frank's office—where, so he said, he had remained, undisturbed by any sounds in the corridor, for some six hours after Mary Phagan's visit—appears to have decided the police that he should be taken into custody for further questioning.

Within a few days the case against him was greatly strengthened by a statement—an amalgam of earlier statements, though with inconsistencies between them ironed out—made by James Conley, a young, semiliterate black man who worked as a sweeper and odd-job man at the factory. Conley, who had certainly been in the building when Mary Phagan went there, claimed that Frank had summoned him to the metal room, shown him the girl's dead body, and ordered him to help carry it to the basement, using the elevator. Conley also stated that he had written the two notes at Frank's dictation, and that Frank had given him two hundred dollars and then taken the money back, saying that he would return it in a day or so.

The announcement that Frank had been charged with the murder was seen by some Atlantans as a fine excuse for showing off their prejudice against the entire Jewish race. Not that any of them needed further excuse, but that was provided by newspaper reports—which may have been incorrect—that rich Jews were contributing toward the defense costs. During the thirty days of the trial, crowds outside the courthouse chanted anti-Semitic slogans; the prosecutors were cheered, the defense attorneys jostled and threatened that "if the Jew don't hang, we'll hang *you*." Local papers enflamed the prejudice. When Conley did not merely withstand a long and searching cross-examination but responded to thoughtless questions from defense council by saying that he had often stood sentry outside Frank's office while the manager performed indecent sexual acts with girls who worked at the factory, an editorialist declared that Mary Phagan had been "pursued to a hideous death by this filthy perverted Jew from New York." The jury took four hours to decide that Frank was guilty, and he was sentenced to death.

Leo Frank Defense Committees were formed in various northern cities. Well over a million people, by no means all of them Jewish, signed petitions urging the governor of Georgia, John Slaton, to commute the death sentence to life imprisonment. Frank's lawyers argued his case before one court of appeal after another. William J. Burns, founder of the largest private-investigation company in America, was hired to seek out facts that could be used in aid of the contention that the murder might have been committed by James Conley. Shortly before the end of Governor Slaton's term of office, Burns, who stood accused of having given bribes for perjured testimony, obtained a statement from a former girlfriend of Conley in which she said that he had told her that he had committed the murder; she also swore that a sheaf of "obscene and lecherous" notes appended to the statement had been written to her by Conley while he was serving a year's sentence in a chain gang for being an accessory after the fact of the crime. Although he, in turn, swore that he had neither confessed nor written the notes (handwriting analyses failed to resolve the latter controversy), the governor concluded that the notes were "powerful evidence in behalf of the defendant" and granted a reprieve. Before the decision was made public, Frank had been taken in secret to the state prison farm at Milledgeville, a hundred miles southeast of Atlanta.

Two months later, in the middle of August 1915, a gang of men calling themselves the Knights of Mary Phagan congregated around her grave. After reciting Christian prayers, they vowed vengeance. On Monday, August 16, twenty-five of the knights drove to the prison farm and, unhampered by armed guards, abducted Leo Frank from the hospital, where he was recovering from neck wounds inflicted by a fellow prisoner. He was taken to Marietta—to a copse where Mary Phagan had played as a small child.

Oddly enough, considering that an alarm message was telegraphed to the authorities in Atlanta within an hour of the abduction and that the journey from Milledgeville to Marietta took some eight hours, the lynching party reached its destination without having been noticed by a single policeman along the route. The knights "performed a duty to Southern womanhood and to Southern society" by hanging Frank from an oak tree (which, within a few days, was chipped down to its roots by souvenir hunters). Also oddly enough, given that prints of snaps showing the knights standing below the suspended corpse sold like hotcakes in Georgia, no one was ever prosecuted.

During the next seventy years, Jewish writers and Jewish organizations (at least one of which was an offshoot from a Leo Frank Defense Committee) sought to increase the number of gentiles who believed that Frank had been found guilty of the murder of Mary Phagan simply because he was a Jew. In 1982 Alonzo Mann, who was then eighty-three, told reporters that he had been an office boy at the National Pencil Company in 1913 (which was true) and that, in the early afternoon of that year's Confederate Memorial Day, he had gone to the factory for some reason and had seen James Conley, alone, carrying Mary Phagan's body to a trapdoor to the basement. Conley, he said, had told him, "If you ever mention this, I'll kill you." Now, he said, he wanted to clear both his conscience and Leo Frank's name.

Three Jewish organizations got together and petitioned Georgia's Board of Pardons and Paroles, arguing that Mann's statement gave grounds for the pardoning of Frank. At the end of 1983 the board reported: "After an exhaustive review and many hours of deliberation, it is impossible to decide conclusively the guilt or innocence of Leo M.

Frank." The Jewish organizations tried again, this time arguing that they should not have to prove Frank's innocence, "only that he was denied justice," and in the spring of 1986, after the governor had "expressed concern over . . . the very sensitive issue" to the board, a pardon was granted on the grounds that "the State failed to protect Mr. Frank and because officials failed to bring his killers to justice."

I agree that an act of atonement for the unpunished lynching was long overdue, but I fail to see the slightest logic in the notion that a man can be cleared of a crime because a crime was subsequently committed against him. One can see the Georgia board's dilemma: if they, choosing to forget the inconclusive result of their review of the evidence in the Mary Phagan case, had said that the trial verdict was wrong, they would, in effect, have said that James Conley was the murderer, and that would have tossed them from the frying pan into the fire, for there are quite as many black organizations as there are Jewish ones.

The pardoning of Leo Frank is less peculiar than an action taken in 1977 by the governor of Massachusetts, Michael Dukakis, with regard to Nicola Sacco and Bartolomeo Vanzetti, who were executed in 1927, six years after they were convicted of the murder during a payroll robbery of a cashier, Frederick Parmenter, and a guard, Alessandro Berardelli. Although Governor Dukakis insisted that he "took no stand" on whether Sacco and Vanzetti were innocent or guilty, he declared August 23, the anniversary of the executions, a memorial day in their honor.

In the light of the Georgia board's pardoning and the Massachusetts governor's honoring, I shouldn't be surprised if, before long, as an indirect consequence of the plague of potty-theory books about the assassination of President Kennedy, Lee Harvey Oswald is formally acquitted of his crime for no better reason than that he himself was murdered by Jack Ruby.

In Washington, D.C.

I traveled through a night (and through both of the Carolinas and Virginia) to Washington's Union Station, which is a lovely Edwardian place, quite as grand as Grand Central and rather cleaner. The balcony around the concourse is lined with three dozen statues of Roman legionnaires. Their skirtlessness so shocked the first stationmaster that he insisted that each set of solid genitalia be hidden behind a shield, and the resultant pleasing effect is of a bevy of muscular but bijou-breasted fan-dancers in funny hats. Disgracefully, a double-decker restaurant, which would be an eyesore anywhere, even in a scrap-metal yard, has been stuck bang in the middle of the splendid concourse, as if with the intention of spoiling the view.

The less said about my hotel, the better. At the very time I was there, it was reported in the press that the entire chain of hotels of which this is one had been sold, and I am almost as sure that the new owners will have made changes at the Washington branch as I am that no change could possibly have made things worse. The reception clerks were disheveled, unhelpful, and inefficient to the extent that my request for cash in exchange for a fifty-dollar travelers' check was turned down, without a word or look of apology, because the till was bare; I had to hope that the rumpled sheets and pillow slips on my bed had not been ironed rather than not been changed; the overhead light in

Union Station, Washington, D.C.

the bathroom gave out more heat than illumination, and as a mat made of something like emery board was, inexplicably, glued in the bath, it was necessary to sit stock-still while bathing or risk scraping of the scrotum; and—the last straw, this—when I went to the so-called restaurant, meaning to have breakfast there, I was informed by the only waiter energetic enough to totter from his chair to my table that the chef could not make toast.

In Washington the cost of a cab ride depends on the number of zones through which the cab has passed; the system, similar to that on the London Underground, not only does away with meters, which can be rigged, but also encourages the drivers to take shortcuts and, therefore, it seems to me, should be introduced in other cities, English as well as American. The cabbie who drove me from Union Station to the hotel waited while I booked in and then took me to the incredibly ugly headquarters of the FBI, getting me there just in time to join the other people, twenty or so, who also had arranged to go on the public-relations tour.

I must say that I was quite bored throughout the first part of the tour (lots of placards outlining the history and the present structure and activities of the bureau—one of the said-to-be two Dillinger death masks was on display) and slightly embarrassed during the second part, when, like visitors at a zoo, we looked through windows, which I hoped were of one-way glass, at people working in various forensic-science laboratories. While concentrating more on the panes than on the activities behind them, I recalled the fact that, only hours before the recent grand opening of a hotel in London, someone just happened to notice that the last-minute rush to get the foyer ready had resulted in the one-way glass forming a whole wall of the gents' room being inserted the wrong way round—and that fact reminded me of another: that the marketing department of a multinational frozen-food corporation was preparing to launch a product as "Battered Cod Pieces" till someone, perhaps descended from the first stationmaster of Washington's Union Station, blushed at the double meaningness of the description. My conclusion that busybodies like those two are also spoilsports caused me to wonder whether any Americans have ever used the word *busybody* as it is still, though rarely, used in England, as the name for a mirror set next to a lace-curtained window so as to reflect passersby.

Prior to the FBI tour's finale, I was the only one who asked the guide, a well-briefed slip of a girl, any questions (I learned, among other things, two concerning women: that none had been accepted as an agent till 1972, after the death of J. Edgar Hoover, and that though the bureau had been publishing lists of "Ten Most Wanted Fugitives" for well over half a century, only some ten women have achieved inclusion)—but I think I was the only one who did not join in the question-and-answer session after an agent had talked to us about handguns, illustrating certain points by firing different weapons at pictures of people. Two little old ladies, one with blue hair in a net and both wearing pretty flower-patterned frocks, seemed to be more knowledgeable about the relative harmfulness of types of .22 automatic pistol than the agent was. As the explosions had given me a bit of a headache, I was pleased when the tour ended and I could breathe fresh air.

I often lost my way in Washington, and my confusion must have been apparent on at least three occasions, when I was offered directions to wherever I couldn't find. It is sadly true that because I had been approached by so many beggars in every place I had visited excepting Kent and Benson, I had come to assume that anyone who approached me would be cadging cash or cigarettes; and so, suspicious that any voluntary offer of help would lead to a hard-luck story, I dashed away from each of the three helpful persons the minute I knew which way to go, saying perfunctory thanks over my shoulder. By the end of my visit to America's capital city, which is quite as scrounger-littered as London, I had gathered that its beggars were of a more sedentary disposition than those elsewhere, for the undoubtable ones I noticed, all in the midtown pedestrian precincts that provide the easiest pickings, remained seated while muttering their appeals at no one in particular, expecting sightseers to go to the trouble of approaching *them*.

I went into several buildings, including that of the Supreme Court. Lovely and white both inside and out, it impressed me even more than I had expected it to. (I suppose one could say that, like the old *Punch* magazine, the nine-person Supreme Court is not as good as it used to be, following that comment with another—"It never *was*"— but there is surely cause for concern that the Court has been degraded in recent years by the appointment of justices *solely* on account of their party politics or ethnic background.) I pottered around just a couple of the thirteen museums of the Smithsonian Institution (which, I must patriotically point out, was founded by an Englishman who never set foot in America) and bought a Smithsonian-prepared set of four audio tapes, *American Musical Theater:* original-cast recordings of hit songs from shows produced on Broadway between 1898 and 1964, since when there have been no more than a few memorable American-made musicals. And, of course, I visited Ford's Theater and, across the street, the Petersen House, in which President Lincoln died after being shot by John Wilkes Booth while attending a benefit performance of the English comedy *Our American Cousin* at the theater on the night of Good Friday 1865.

I'm not sure, though I've given it some thought, that the assassination of Abraham Lincoln is any business of mine—mine as a crime historian, I mean—or, for that matter, that any political assassination is. I have the feeling that such events are not, as crime writers whom I detest would certainly say, Murder Writ Large; I don't think that the word *murder* is sufficient to them. At least the killing of Lincoln was not done by a complete nonentity or an absolute lunatic, as are just about all of the singular killings that alter a nation's destiny. John Wilkes Booth stands out as being of a better class of assassin than any others I can think of since the latter days of Cassius and Brutus. (I agree with those

two very good crime novelists, the American Rex Stout and the British Josephine Tey, that the case against King Richard III for the killing of the princes in the Tower, is as shaky as jello. There ought to be a verb, "to

Shake-spear," meaning to gouge out any virtues in a dead person so that he can be pictured as a thoroughly villainous character in a historical play or in a book, whether fact-inspired fictional or allegedly factual.)

Almost as many theories have been fabricated about the assassination of President Lincoln as about the assassination of President Kennedy, but the most influentially deceitful of them have been shown up by William Hanchett in his book *The Lincoln Murder Conspiracies* (1983). I wish someone as lucid as Hanchett would similarly take a hammer to the Kennedy crackpottery.

While I was in Cleveland, Albert Borowitz told me something that intrigued me on two counts, one being that it reveals that the climactic scene in the movie *The Man Who Knew Too Much*, made twice by Hitchcock, is an instance of art imitating history. The other is that Booth, an actor, used a tidbit of theatrical knowledge in aid of his crime. During the second scene of the third act of *Our American Cousin*, the character called Asa, left alone on stage, has one of the biggest laugh lines—or rather, laugh *words*—in the play: calling after a character who has just exited, Asa says, "I guess I know enough to turn you inside out, old gal—you sockdologising [exceptional] old man trap." The word *sockdologising*, which never failed to have the audience rolling in the aisles, roaring loud enough to deaden the sound of a pistol shot, was taken by Booth as his cue to open the door of the box on the right of the stage and instantly shoot the president through the back of the head. It is a pleasing irony that, in jumping from the box, he, a sockdologising Confederate, became entangled in Union bunting and fell in such ungainly fashion on the stage that he broke a leg (I wonder if that is the back-to-front origination of the good-luck saying used by American stage actors), thereby spoiling his exit and making horse riding so uncomfortable that he was unable to travel far before being ambushed by Union troops.

The theater building was less than two years old, the replacement of John T. Ford's first theater, made from a church, which had burned down. Ford planned to reopen the theater after the period of mourning for the president but, forced by public outcry and political pressure to change his mind, sold it to the government, which turned it into offices, at first for dealing with military records. In 1893 part of the third floor (presumably the part that had been built on to the upper

"The President's Box."

circle) collapsed, killing or injuring many civil servants. The building was used as a warehouse for government publications till 1932, when it was turned into the Lincoln Museum. Starting in 1946, bills were introduced in Congress to restore Ford's Theater, and, after eighteen years, one was passed that provided the peculiarly exact sum of $2,073,600 (but no extra cents) for that purpose. On Monday, February 12, 1968, when the theater reopened with a performance of a pageant-style play about the Civil War, the then secretary of the interior, Stewart Udall, splendidly ended a speech of welcome by saying: "Here some, unhoping, will find hope; some, grieving, will discover gaiety; and many, weary, will rest. I believe Mr. Lincoln would have wanted it this way."

I had meant to see a show there, but the theater was between productions. Perhaps that was as well, for I doubt if any rehearsed drama on that stage could keep my eyes, my thoughts, from wandering. I sat in the empty auditorium for a while, and invented ghosts.

It is dark outside. Barring delays, this train, called a Metroliner, will arrive at Penn Station, Manhattan, in an hour or so. To all intents and purposes, my journey is over. After I get home next week, when I have deciphered most of the scribbles that began in the Taj Mahal Tandoori's giveaway notebook, which I very nearly lost before I set off, looked at those snaps I have taken that bear resemblance to whatever I pointed my Sure Shot at, and rummaged among the paltry souvenirs that by now must have doubled the weight of my suitcase, I shall be able to concoct general conclusions from the particular things I have seen and heard and felt. Oh yes, I shall be able to.

But I am sure that I will not want to, will not do so. Rather, I shall hope to keep the special memories special, bright inside my head, untarnished by association with other special memories. And anyway (I am trying to be truthful about myself, which is difficult as I have only a sketchy idea of what makes me *me*), though better writers, or writers better at confusing a single swallow with an entire summer, may be capable of giving apriority credence, I don't think I could attempt that without looking sheepish . . . or indeed shifty, for I suspect that my contempt for pundits—criminological, psychiatrical, even, among others, theological—who inflate exceptional happenings into generalizations has become my own generalization that practically all generalizations need to be taken with a pinch of salt. And—talking of salt brings this to mind—I believe that trying to make a few-sentences sense of my past few weeks would be as futile as trying to explain the taste of a tossed salad by analyzing its ingredients, condiments, and dressing. A lot of things that *can* be done (like creating "more useful" animals such as beefalos; banning person-descriptive terms; or making jury service so democratic that there is nothing theoretically wrong with the outcome of separate dozens of people who don't know the difference between forensic fact and televised fiction) should *not* be done.

There: I have made a point. Not much of one, however, since it applies as much in my own country as here. Perhaps there is a point in its near pointlessness—that the concerns of some English people, our hopes and fears, are no different from those of some Americans. We—the ocean-separated lots of some English people and some Americans—are, thank the Lord, still very much alike. In a funny sort of way, we share a patriotism.

I am wearing a souvenir, the only one that is not bulging and untidying my suitcase. A glossy pin-on button that was given to me by the black salesgirl in the bookshop at Ford's Theater. "Take Pride in America," the button says. It seems perfectly natural to me that, though I am English, I do.

Index

books mentioned: *Ben Hur,* by W. Lew, 149; *Bleak House,* 11; *The Crime and Trial of Leopold and Loeb,* by M. McKernan, 56; *Doomed Ship,* by J. Gray, 21; *Double Indemnity,* by J. M. Cain, 21; *Dr. Sam Johnson, Detector,* 12; *Gorse Trilogy,* by P. Hamilton, 12; *The Great Gatsby,* 11–12; *Guinness Book of Records,* 44; *The Killing of Julia Wallace,* by Goodman, xi; on Kent State shootings, 32–33; *The Lincoln Murder Conspiracies,* by W. Hanchett, 187; *Lucia in London,* by E. F. Benson, 142; *The Man Who Never Was,* by E. Montagu, 146; *Psmith Journalist,* by P. G. Wodehouse, 172; *Report of the City Council Committee on Crime of the City of Chicago,* 80; *The Slaying of Joseph Bowne Elwell,* by Goodman, 3
Booth, John Wilkes, 185, 187
Borden, Miss Lizzie, xiii, 71
Borowitz, Albert, 24–27, 34–37, 39, 42–44, 46–47, 187
Borowitz, Helen, 24–27, 34–36, 47
Borowitz, Peter, 26–27
Borowitz True Crime Collection, 26
Boswell, James, 12, 13
Brady, Matthew, 128
Brice, Fanny (Fannie), 4, 92
Broadway Theater, Denver, 92
Brothers, Leo, 64–65
Brown, Michael, 71, 72–73
Brown Palace Hotel, Denver, 85–86, 89, 91, 93, 97–98
Burnaby, Evelyn, 172
Burns, William J., 179
Butterfield Stagecoach, 143

cabbies: in Atlanta, 170; in Chicago, 79; in Cleveland, 24–25; in Denver, 85, 87; Hurshell in Chicago, 53–54, 57, 65–66, 69, 73–74; in San Francisco, 116, 123; in Washington, 183
cabs: in Atlanta, 173; none in Benson, 140; in London, 97; in San Francisco, 112, 116
Cain, James M., 21
Campaign for Real Ale, 133
Cantor, Eddie, 4
Capone, Al, 42, 57–69, 114
Capra, Frank, 21
Carroll, Lewis, 37
Cartland, Barbara, 100–101
Case of the Silent Witnesses, the, 107–8. *See also* Genovese, Kitty, murder case
Cassidy, Butch, 105
Cermak, Anton, 60
Chandler, Raymond, 21
Chaplin, Charlie, 126
Chapman, George (Jack the Ripper?), 44–45
Chapman, Mark, 36
Charles the Clipper, 45–46
Chicago Historical Society, 79–80
Christian Endeavor Society, San Francisco, 120–21
Clanton, Ike and Billy, 143
Clay, Henry, statue, New Orleans, 162, 166
Cleveland Museum of Art, 25
Colbert, Claudette, 112
Colosimo, "Big Jim," 57–58
Condon, J. F., "Jafsie," 8
Conley, James, 178–79, 181
Copeland, George, 94–96
copycat killing, 42
Coward, Noel, 135
crime: collection, 26; history, 56, 80, 172, 187; novelists, 186; on TV, 115–16
Crippen murder case, xiii
Crosby, Bing, 129
Czolgosz, Leon, 22

Hindman, Leslie, auctioneers, 74
historical societies: Atlanta, 175; Benson, Arizona, 142; Chicago, 79–80; Cleveland Police, 37; Denver, 87
Historic New Orleans Collection, 154
Hitchcock, Alfred, movies, 9, 52; *The Man Who Knew Too Much*, 187; *North by Northwest*, 9, 139; *Strangers on a Train*, 11, 21
Hoffa, James Riddle, 28
Holliday, John Henry, "Doc," 103, 142, 143
Hollywood, 127, 128, 136
Hoover, J. Edgar, 74, 184
Hopper, Edward, 133
Horseshoe Saloon, Benson, 141, 145
Howard, Cornelius, 124
Hugo, Victor, 39
Hunt, Corinne, 87, 97
Hussey, Robert and K, 131–32

International Polygonics, 12

Jack the Ripper, 41; in Benson, 144–45; Ripperology, 44–45, 152
Jewish organizations, 180–81
Johnson, Molly, 157, 161
Johnston, General Joseph, 175
Jolson, Al, 111, 129

Kallogh, Isaac, 117
Keaton, Buster, 127
Kefauver, Estes, 168
Keller, Dean and Pat, xii, 26–27, 34–35, 101
Kemmler, William, 22
Kennedy, President John, 27, 182, 187
Kent State University, 26–33
Kingsbury Run, the Mad Butcher of, 38–45
Knickerbocker Hotel, Chicago, 47, 53–54, 62, 73, 80
Knights of Mary Phagan, 180

Kobler, John, 60–61
Krause, Allison, 31

Lamont, Blanche, 119–21
Lancaster, Burt, 115
Langtry, Lillie, "Jersey Lily," 150
language: English versus American, 74–79; euphemism, 101
Las Vegas, 145–46, 150
Lee, Gypsy Rose, 38
Lennon, John, 36
Leopold, Nathan "Babe," 54–57
Lexington Hotel, Chicago, 60–62, 136
Liberace Museum, Las Vegas, 150
Lincoln, President Abraham, 153, 185, 187
Lincoln Avenue, no. 2433, Chicago, 69, 79
Lincoln Museum, Washington, D.C., 188
Lindbergh kidnapping case, 8
Lingle, Alfred "Jake," 62–63
Liverpool Playhouse, ix–x
Loeb, Richard, 54–57
London: beggars in, 124–25, 185; Charing Cross, 62; doubledeckers, 97; Holloway, xiii; Inn of Court, 37; Marble Arch, 1; Oxford Circus, xiii; Piccadilly Circus, 62; South Kensington, 66; St. Catherine's dock, 36; tall buildings and number 13, 2; Underground, 183; Whitechapel, 41
Long, Earl Huey P., "Kingfisher," 152, 161
Lumpkin, Martha, 175

MacArthur, Charles, 8
Mafia, the, 163–68
Magnificent Mile, Chicago, 65–66
Mallory, George Leigh, 158
Manhattan, 21, 151, 162; and Bien Jolie Corset Company, 13; and Carnegie Hall, 5; Isabelle Springer in, 88–89, 97; John Lennon in, 36; and the number 13, 1; Penn Station, 2–4, 8, 15
Mann, Alonzo, 180

places along the way: Bogalusa, 150; Bryan, 52; Buckhead, 175; Donner Lake, 110–11; Dragon Pass, 143; Eaton, 85; Elyria, 52; Gary, Indiana, 53; Hattiesburg, 171; Helper, 104; Hygiene, 85; Lake Pontchartrain, 170; Last Chance, 85; Laurel, 171; Meridian, 171; mission towns, 134–35, 150; New Iberia, 152; Picayune, 171; South Bend, 53; Truckee, 110; Truth or Consequences, 149; Windsor, 85; Winnemucca, 105

Plaza Café, Benson, 142, 147

Polillo, Florence, 42

Pontchartrain Hotel, New Orleans, 153; Bayou Bar, 153, 169

Powell, William, 71

Preservation Hall, New Orleans, 168

prisons: Alcatraz, 113–15, 125; Bodmin, Cornwall, 114; Newgate, London, 1; Parish, New Orleans, 166–67; San Quentin, 123; Sing Sing, 19

Prohibition Bureau, 42

Provenzano Gang, New Orleans, 163–65. *See also* Mafia, the

Punch magazine, 185

Purvis, Melvin, 71–72

Quail Hollow Motel, Benson, 141–42, 145, 148

Queens Village, New York, 15–17

rail travel, 6–8, 21. *See also* trains

Rail Passenger Corporation. *See* Amtrak

Raine, George and Kay, 112–13, 132–33

Rand McNally Atlas, 110

Rappe, Virginia, 127

Republican National Convention, Cleveland, 42

Rhodes, James, 29

Rio Grande River, 149

Riviera, Geraldo, 61–62

Rocky Mountains, 84, 100

Rogers, Will, 4

Roosevelt, President-elect Franklin Delano, 60

ROTC (Reserve Officers Training Corps), 29–30, 32

route guides. *See* guidebooks

Rowland, John, 172

Royal Philharmonic Orchestra, 101–2

Royal Marines, 146

Ruby, Jack, 182

Russell, Ken, 21

Russell, Commissioner, Chicago, 63–64

S-M-C Cartage Company. *See* St. Valentine's Day Massacre

Sacco, Nicola, 182

Sage, Anna, 71–72

Salieri, Antonio, 169

Salt Lake City, Utah, 104–5

Sandburg, Carl, 82

San Simeon, 135

Scheuer, Sandra, 31

Schroeder, William, 31

serial killers, 44. *See also* Jack the Ripper; Kingsbury Run, Mad Butcher of

Settle, Ronnie, 101

Shakers, 24

Shakespeare, William, 1, 172

Shakspeare, Joseph, 164–66

Sherry-Netherland Hotel, New York, 151

shows mentioned: *American Musical Theater* audio tapes, 185; *The Boys from Syracuse*, 35; *Call Me Madam*, 35; *Damn Yankees*, 35; *Fiorello!* 35; *Follies*, 92–94; *Mamzelle Champagne*, 3; *Midnight Frolics*, by Ziegfeld, 4; *On Your Toes*, 35; *Our American Cousin*, 185, 187; *Outward Bound*, 105; *The Pajama Game*, 35; *Pal Joey*, 35; *Private Lives*, 36; *Turandot*, 140; West End productions, x

Silverman, David, 74

Slaton, John, 179